W9-BBX-599

The
Big Book of
Homemade Products
FOR
YOUR ## SKIN, HEALTH & HOME

EASY, ALL-NATURAL
DIY PROJECTS USING HERBS,
FLOWERS & OTHER PLANTS

Jan Berry

FOUNDER *of* THE BLOG THE NERDY FARM WIFE

PAGE STREET
PUBLISHING CO.

Dedication

To my husband and children, who are my best friends and biggest fans. Thank you for always cheering me on and being patient while "The Book" consumed our lives for a season. Now that it's done, I promise more lazy creek days and homemade ice cream, and less computer time and baked chicken (again?!) for supper.

PAGE STREET
PUBLISHING CO.

Copyright © 2020 Jan Berry

First published in 2020 by
Page Street Publishing Co.
27 Congress Street, Suite 105
Salem, MA 01970
www.pagestreetpublishing.com

All rights reserved. No part of this book may be reproduced or used, in any form or by any means, electronic or mechanical, without prior permission in writing from the publisher.

Distributed by Macmillan, sales in Canada by The Canadian Manda Group.

24   23   22   21   3   4   5

ISBN-13: 978-1-64567-001-8
ISBN-10: 1-64567-001-5

Library of Congress Control Number: 2019942717

Cover and book design by Laura Benton for Page Street Publishing Co.
Photography by Jan Berry

Printed and bound in China

Page Street Publishing protects our planet by donating to nonprofits like The Trustees, which focuses on local land conservation.

Contents

Introduction

When I wrote the first edition of this book, it was focused on showcasing creative
and practical ways to use common flowers and herbs that grow right around us.
Teaching others how to put to good use an unruly lemon balm patch or an out-of-control
mint plant is a personal passion that has only grown in the ensuing years since that first
book was born.

In this freshly updated and expanded version, you'll find those same favorite
projects, plus even more herbs and flowers to explore, additional formulas to help
you create your own recipes from scratch, as well as 50 new recipes to inspire your
imagination.

You'll learn how to grab a rose from your garden, a handful of dandelions from your
backyard or a bunch of herbs from the local farmer's market and make something
beautiful, useful and good for you, your family and your home. Most of the projects
make delightful gifts for loved ones too!

While the recipes in the book are heavily centered around flowers and herbs, don't
let that be a hindrance if you don't have easy access to plants. Infused oils can be
swapped out for plain oils, and most of the flowers and herbs can be interchanged
or even omitted in some cases. For more about this, see the Substitution Tips
section on page 25.

Because I live on a tight budget and Internet shipping costs a small fortune, it's
important to me to use as many locally sourced ingredients as I can. When you live
in rural America like I do, the store options are slim, but I'm still able to find most of
my ingredients within a 30-mile (48-km) radius. For the things that have to be
ordered online, I've listed some of my favorite vendors in the Resources section (page 330)
in the back of this book.

You'll find that the recipes and instructions are pretty straightforward, but if you run
into any question or problem, please contact me at thenerdyfarmwife.com and I'll be
happy to help.

Now if you're ready to make some fun stuff with me, turn the page and let's get started!

Jan Berry

Getting Started Making Natural, Homemade Products

Common Herbs & Flowers & Their Benefits

Our gardens and backyards are filled with flowers, herbs and weeds that have the potential to provide many fun and useful products for home, health and beauty. If you can safely eat a plant, there's a good chance that it can be used in other interesting ways as well.

Although I've listed details about the ones specifically used to make the projects in this book, this isn't an all-inclusive list of plants with benefits. Explore the Internet, your library and local bookstore to find articles and books about herbs and edible flowers that grow in your area. Some common plants, such as roses and basil, are easily recognizable, but always be certain in the identification of what you're harvesting before use.

Arnica (*Arnica montana*) is an anti-inflammatory herb that's excellent for treating bruising, sore muscles, arthritis and pulled muscles. Don't use on open wounds.

➤ Cayenne & Ginger Arthritis Balm—page 74

➤ Muscle Aches Salve—page 66

➤ Saint John's Wort, Arnica & Calendula Trauma Oil—page 267

Basil (*Ocimum basilicum*) has anti-inflammatory, antioxidant, antibacterial and tick-repelling properties. Taken orally, it has an analgesic (pain relieving) effect on chronic pain conditions and makes a good expectorant in cough syrups. Basil opens up the sinuses, helps headaches, can be used in baths for stress or pain, as a toner for acne, rubbed on bug bites, incorporated in a salve for joint aches and has even been shown in one study to be effective in an antiaging cream. In short, basil is not just for pesto!

➤ Basil & Rose Kombucha Toner—page 50

➤ Basil & Lime Lip Balm—page 178

➤ Create Your Own Vinegar Hair Rinse—page 211

➤ Catnip & Basil Insect Repellant Spray—page 257

➤ Basil Mint Sore Throat Spray—page 275

Bee Balm (*Monarda fistulosa*) leaves and flowers can be infused in oil and used to treat wounds and achy muscles. They're also antibacterial and helpful for sore throats and colds.

➤ Menthol Chest Balm—page 77

➤ Bee Balm Intensive Hand Butter—page 88

➤ Bee Balm & Lemon Cough Syrup—page 272

➤ Yarrow & Bee Balm Antiseptic Wash—page 315

Calendula (*Calendula officinalis*) is a well-loved and often used flower that's included in many skin-care recipes. It's a classic addition to diaper creams for babies, due to its anti-inflammatory, antibacterial and skin-healing properties. It may help conditions such as eczema, is a lymphatic (helps relieve congested lymph nodes), is good for sore throats and swollen tonsils, helps skin regenerate and is used in formulations to reduce the swelling and appearance of varicose veins. The tea can be used as an antiseptic wound wash. It should not be used internally by pregnant women.

➤ Anti-Acne Herbal Tea—page 47

➤ Charcoal Drawing Balm—page 78

➤ Triple Sunshine Body Butter—page 87

➤ Belly Butter for Expecting Moms—page 93

➤ Calendula Whipped Coconut Oil—page 94

➤ Calendula Whipped Coconut Butter—page 97

➤ Basic Calendula Lotion—page 111

➤ Calendula Oatmeal Bath Bombs—page 133

➤ Calendula Spice Fizzing Bath Salts—page 146

➤ Calendula Spice & Honey Cleansing Scrub—page 157

➤ Calendula Orange Blossom Scrub—page 167

➤ Herbal Hair Health Tea—page 198

➤ Dry Shampoo for Light Hair Tones—page 205

➤ Coconut & Calendula Conditioning Rinse—page 212

➤ Carrot & Calendula Soap—page 246

➤ Bug Bite Powder—page 261

➤ Saint John's Wort, Arnica & Calendula Trauma Oil—page 267

➤ Itchy Skin Rinse—page 320

➤ All-Purpose Animal Salve—page 323

Catnip (*Nepeta cataria*) is a cooling and drying herb. It repels mosquitoes and flies, is a mild analgesic (pain reliever), calms the nerves so a person can rest, is added to bath soaks to relieve stress and can be used in a hair rinse for dandruff. As a tea it may help relieve colds, coughs, upset stomach, nausea, toothache and headache.

- Create Your Own Vinegar Hair Rinse—page 211
- Catnip & Basil Insect Repellant Spray—page 257

Cayenne (*Capsicum annuum*) is a very warming spice used externally to block pain receptors. It's used in salves and other products for arthritis, sore muscles and general aches and pains.

- Cayenne & Ginger Arthritis Balm—page 74
- Warm Toes Lotion Bar—page 105

Chamomile (*Matricaria chamomilla*) is antibacterial, antifungal, antiseptic and anti-inflammatory. Chamomile has been shown to have a mild cortisone-like effect and is often used in lotions, creams, salves and other products to help relieve rashes, irritated or red skin and eczema.

- Chamomile Honey Face Wash—page 38
- Triple Sunshine Body Butter—page 87
- Honey & Chamomile Cream—page 122
- Sleepy Time Bath Bombs—page 134
- Calming Bath Soak—page 144
- Lavender Sleepy Time Bath Tea—page 149
- Lemon Chamomile Bath Melts—page 156
- Chamomile Brown Sugar Scrub Cubes—page 172
- Chamomile Lip Scrub—page 185
- Chamomile "Almost Castile" Soap—page 226
- Chamomile Calming Syrup—page 285
- Stress Relief Massage Oil—page 286

Chickweed (*Stellaria media*) is a nourishing weed that pops up in early spring. It's used to promote lymph flow, relieve aching joints and as a skin-soothing agent for eczema and itchy skin conditions.

- Chickweed & Violet Salve—page 65
- Oatmeal & Chickweed Eczema Cream—page 118
- Spring Detox Deodorant—page 265

Cornflower (*Centaurea cyanus*) is also called Bachelor Button. The flower extract is used as a skin conditioner and astringent. The petals add color to teas or bath soaks and contain anti-inflammatory properties. A finely filtered tea can be used to soothe eye irritation and to reduce puffiness.

- Lavender Blue Mask—page 58

Daisy (Oxeye, *Leucanthemum vulgare*; common or English, *Bellis perennis*) is a common weed found in fields and on roadsides. Don't harvest plants from roadsides, as they can be contaminated with heavy metals and runoff. Shasta daisies (*Leucanthemum × superbum*) from the garden work equally well in body care recipes. Daisies were known in the past as a traditional wound herb for bruises, broken bones, eczema, inflammation and infection. In more recent years they have been the subject of a study that scientifically verified their wound-healing abilities.

- Daisy Vanilla Lip Balm—page 181
- Flea-Repelling Vinegar Rinse—page 316

Dandelion (*Taraxacum officinale*) may be vilified by those who seek a perfectly green lawn each spring, but it is an important plant in a multitude of beneficial ways. The flowers are enjoyed by a variety of pollinators and insect life. They are also a good source of lecithin, and when infused in oil and turned into salves, lotions and creams, act as a mild analgesic (pain reliever) and healing agent for painful, chapped skin. The plant tincture stimulates the liver and has been known to clear acne and eczema when taken internally over time. It has also been studied for its cancer-fighting potential. Traditionally, dandelion sap has been used to treat microbial or fungal skin infections along with acne and warts.

- Dandelion Thyme Vinegar Toner & Tonic—page 48
- Muscle Aches Salve—page 66
- Dandelion Cuticle Balm—page 82
- Triple Sunshine Body Butter—page 87
- Dandelion Body Butter—page 90
- Dandelion Orange Fizzy Bath Melts—page 160
- Floral Salt Foot Scrub Bars—page 171
- Dandelion Plantain Chapped Lip Treatment—page 181
- Dandelion Scrub Bar—page 244
- Spring Detox Deodorant—page 265
- Lavender Dandelion Pain Relief Oil—page 268
- Dandelion Magnesium Lotion—page 283

Dianthus (*Dianthus* spp) is an ornamental bedding plant, with flowers in shades of white, pink and red and are also called "pinks." The edible flowers can be used as a garnish, but I primarily use them in body-care recipes as a natural colorant for bath salts and sugar scrubs.

- Floral Salt Foot Scrub Bars—page 171

Elderflowers (*Sambucus nigra*) help heal wounds and have been used for generations as an aid to obtaining a beautiful complexion. The berries of this shrub are a proven treatment for influenza.

- Wildflowers in May Lotion—page 108
- Elderflower Eye Cream—page 124

Forsythia (*Forsythia* spp) is a common, bright yellow flowering shrub whose blooms are among the first signs of spring each year. While the autumn fruits are traditionally the plant part used as medicine, the flowers can be utilized in a similar, milder-acting manner. Forsythia is cooling, anti-inflammatory and combines splendidly with honeysuckle to fight viruses. The flowers can also be used in preparations for acne or skin flare-ups.

- Forsythia Clear Skin Toner—page 45
- Floral Salt Foot Scrub Bars—page 171

Hollyhock (*Alcea* spp) is a cousin to the herb marsh mallow and shares similar soothing, cooling and anti-inflammatory properties. The flowers and leaves can be infused in oil to make salves and creams.

- Hollyhock Split-End Crème—page 197
- Hollyhock Shampoo Bar—page 241

Lavender (*Lavandula angustifolia*) is one of the most loved herbs around. The sweet-scented plant is antibacterial, antifungal, anti-inflammatory, acts to regenerate skin, soothes inflammation, speeds up wound healing, fights infection, repels flies, fleas and moths and freshens laundry. Lavender can be incorporated in a multitude of products for health and home, including salves, creams, lotions, soaps, cleaners and more. While the flowers are most commonly used, the leaves can be utilized in many recipes as well.

- Lavender Castile Soapy Facial Cleanser—page 42
- Lavender Blue Mask—page 58
- Lavender, Coconut & Honey Balm—page 69
- Sleepy Time Lotion—page 112
- Lavender Milk Bath Bombs—page 130
- Garden Herbs Bath Soak—page 143
- Calming Bath Soak—page 144
- Lavender Sleepy Time Bath Tea—page 149
- Lavender Oatmeal Bath Melts—page 153

Lemon Balm (*Melissa officinalis*) is a mild stress reliever, uplifts mood and has a marked antiviral effect, especially against herpes viruses, making it ideal for including in lip balms and salves for cold sores.

Lemongrass (*Cymbopogon citratus*) is a powerhouse of beneficial properties. It's anti-amebic and antibacterial, a decoction of the stalk acts as an antidiarrheal, the infused oil is antifungal, the fresh leaves are antifebrile (a fever reducer), a tea of dried leaves is anti-inflammatory and the essential oil is antimalarial. All that, and it smells wonderful, too!

Mint, Peppermint or Spearmint (*Mentha piperita, Mentha spicata*) is cooling and pain relieving. It can help ease stomachaches, indigestion, headaches, nausea and sore muscles. It's useful in salves for cooling itchy or inflamed skin conditions. While peppermint and spearmint are most commonly used, you can also use orange mint, pineapple mint, apple mint, chocolate mint and other such varieties.

Nettle (*Urtica dioica*) is anti-inflammatory, astringent, healing, antibacterial, antimicrobial, nutritious and can be used externally as a treatment for dandruff and acne. It's included in many hair-care formulations to improve scalp circulation and to stimulate hair growth.

(continued)

- → Herbal Dry Shampoo for Dark Hair Tones—page 205
- → Create Your Own Vinegar Hair Rinse—page 211
- → Nettle & Coconut Oil Vitamin Treats—page 327
- → Tinkle Tonic Broth—page 328

Oregano (*Origanum vulgare*) is powerful against bacteria and fungus, helps fight upper respiratory infections and contains several vitamins, minerals and potent antioxidants. It's a great addition to cold-care remedies.

- → Oregano Oxymel—page 276
- → Four Thieves Vinegar Spray—page 302

Parsley (*Petroselinum crispum*) is best known as a breath freshener. It's nutritious and high in vitamins A, C and K, helps eliminate the uric acid that causes gout and may be beneficial to animals with arthritis.

- → Peppermint & Parsley Fresh-Breath Dog Treats—page 324

Peony (*Paeonia* spp) is an old-fashioned garden flower used in this book as a natural colorant for scrubs and bath salts. Use dark pink or red peonies; the palest pink flowers don't work as well.

- → Peony & Orange Sugar Scrub—page 164
- → Floral Salt Foot Scrub Bars—page 171

Pine (*Pinus strobus*) is high in vitamin C and antioxidants. The resin is antibacterial and helpful for sore, stiff joints and rheumatism. Pine is very warming and increases circulation.

- → Peppermint Pine Headache Salve—page 81
- → Sore Muscle Bath Bags—page 141
- → Garden Herbs Bath Soak—page 143
- → Orange Pine Floor Cleaner—page 305

Plantain (*Plantago major*) is a common weed found in many backyards and driveways. It cools, soothes and moistens and is one of the best herbs for skin irritations, cuts, bug bites and scrapes. For in-field first aid, you can simply grab a leaf from your yard, pulverize it by chewing on it a few seconds, then place it directly on the irritation for relief. Plantain, the green leafy weed, should not be confused with plantain fruit. Plantain makes a very nice infused oil for soaps, salves and lip balms.

- → Cooling Sunburn Cubes—page 54
- → Plantain & Yarrow Heel Balm—page 62
- → Charcoal Drawing Balm—page 78
- → Sleepy Time Lotion—page 112
- → Garden Herbs Bath Soak—page 143
- → Lavender Plantain Scrub—page 167
- → Dandelion Plantain Chapped Lip Treatment—page 181
- → Flea-Repelling Vinegar Rinse—page 316
- → All-Purpose Animal Salve—page 323

Purple Coneflower (*Echinacea purpurea*) is anti-inflammatory and helps soothe insect bites and minor wounds. It readily kills *P. acnes*, which is the main cause of acne vulgaris. Taken internally, it acts as an immune stimulant.

- → Winter Cold Care Lip Butter—page 187
- → Tinkle Tonic Broth—page 328

Rose (*Rosa* spp) is a gentle remedy for inflammation. It's astringent, soothing, cools hot flashes, can be mixed with honey to make a soothing throat syrup and is an excellent addition to skin-care recipes. The scent of rose uplifts the spirits and gladdens the heart.

- → Honey, Rose & Oat Face Cleanser—page 37
- → Basil & Rose Kombucha Toner—page 50
- → Rose Pink Face Mask—page 58

(continued)

- Regenerating Rose Balm—page 73
- Cocoa Rose Lotion Bars—page 103
- Wildflowers in May Lotion—page 108
- Rose Face Cream—page 121
- Fizzy Rose Lemonade Soak—page 147
- Lavender Sleepy Time Bath Tea—page 149
- Vanilla Rose Bath Melts—page 154
- Rose Garden Scrub—page 167
- Floral Salt Foot Scrub Bars—page 171
- Rosy Lip Tint—page 181
- Herbal Dry Shampoo for Medium Hair Tones—page 205
- Old-Fashioned Rose Soap—page 232
- Calamine Rose Lotion—page 262
- Aloe Rose Sunburn & Hot Flash Spray—page 284
- Rose Window Cleaner—page 301
- Itchy Skin Rinse—page 320

Rosemary (*Rosmarinus officinalis*) increases circulation, making it wonderful for use in sore muscle salves and recipes for healthier scalp and hair growth. Just a whiff of rosemary has been shown to increase concentration and focus.

- Garden Herbs Bath Soak—page 143
- Energizing Rosemary Mint Bath Tea—page 149
- Herbal Hair Health Tea—page 198
- Rosemary Beard Oil—page 207
- Extra Mild Soapwort Hair Wash—page 208
- Create Your Own Vinegar Hair Rinse—page 211
- Lemon & Rosemary All-Purpose Cleaning Spray—page 290
- Four Thieves Vinegar Spray—page 302

Sage (*Salvia officinalis*) is warming and drying. It reduces sweating and is a good antimicrobial for sore throats. Because it's such a drying herb, nursing mothers should not ingest more than normal culinary use, or it may negatively affect milk supply.

- Sage Green Mask—page 58
- Garden Herbs Bath Soak—page 143
- Herbal Hair Health Tea—page 198
- Create Your Own Vinegar Hair Rinse—page 211
- Four Thieves Vinegar Spray—page 302

Sunflowers (*Helianthus annuus*) have skin-soothing, anti-inflammatory properties and are used in formulations for shiny hair.

- Sunflower Salve—page 70
- Sunflower Lotion Bars—page 100
- Sunflower & Sweet Orange Cream—page 119
- Sunflower Citrus Scrub—page 159
- Vegan Sunflower Lip Tint—page 181
- Sunflower Hot Oil Treatment—page 201
- Create Your Own Vinegar Hair Rinse—page 211
- Sunflower Shampoo Bar—page 238

Thyme (*Thymus vulgaris*) is a potent disinfectant, making it a good choice for treating cuts, scrapes and sore throats. It's also been shown to be highly effective against the bacteria that cause acne.

- Anti-Acne Herbal Tea—page 47
- Dandelion Thyme Vinegar Toner & Tonic—page 48
- Thyme & Raw Honey Mask—page 57
- Grapeseed & Thyme Lotion—page 116
- Garden Herbs Bath Soak—page 143
- Herbal Hair Health Tea—page 198
- Thyme Flaky Scalp Spray—page 214

- Thyme & Witch Hazel Clear Skin Facial Bar—page 235
- Lemon Thyme Dusting Spray—page 296
- Four Thieves Vinegar Spray—page 302

Violets (*Viola odorata*) are high in vitamins A and C. They're soothing and cooling, help relieve swollen or congested lymph glands and are good for a dry cough and sore throat. Traditionally, violet leaves and flowers have been used in poultices, salves and massage oils for fibrocystic breasts. They're also reputed to ease the pain of headache.

- Violet Flower Cleanser—page 41
- Violet-Infused Aloe—page 51
- Cooling Sunburn Cubes—page 54
- Chickweed & Violet Salve—page 65
- Violet Leaf Lotion Bars—page 102
- Sleepy Time Lotion—page 112
- Oatmeal & Chickweed Eczema Cream—page 118
- Violet & Aloe Moisturizing Cream—page 127
- Garden Herbs Bath Soak—page 143
- Floral Salt Foot Scrub Bars—page 171
- Herbal Hair Health Tea—page 198
- Create Your Own Vinegar Hair Rinse—page 211
- Spring Detox Deodorant—page 265
- Violet Flower Sore Throat Syrup—page 279

Yarrow (*Achillea millefolium*) is antiseptic, astringent and anti-inflammatory. It's helpful for treating cracked and damaged skin.

- Plantain & Yarrow Heel Balm—page 62
- Yarrow & Bee Balm Antiseptic Wash—page 315
- Flea-Repelling Vinegar Rinse—page 316

Preserving Herbs and Flowers

While it's always fun to work with fresh flowers and herbs, unfortunately they just don't stay in season as long as we'd like. They can, however, be dried or frozen for use throughout the rest of the year. Both forms will retain similar medicinal and healthful benefits, although dried offers a wider range of uses and is not reliant upon electricity to stay fresh.

Dried flowers and herbs can be used in all the projects in this book, unless noted otherwise. Frozen flowers and herbs work best for making soaps, vinegars and other water-based projects. Because they contain moisture, they won't mix into oil-based items such as salves, lip balms or body butters.

To dry fresh flowers and leaves, collect them on a preferably sunny mid-morning when their volatile oils are at peak level. Bring them inside and spread them out in a single layer over a clean dishtowel, out of direct sunlight but in a location that gets good air circulation. Turn each piece over once or twice per day until completely dry. Depending on humidity levels and temperature in your house, this could take anywhere from 2 days to a full week.

Some herbs, such as thyme, rosemary, hyssop, dill, parsley, basil, lemon balm and many more, can be hung upside down in small clusters tied together with kitchen twine. Keep them out of direct sunlight and take them down as soon as they dry or they'll fade and get dusty.

For quickest results and very humid climates, you can also use a dehydrator. Remember to keep the temperature less than 110°F (43°C), in order to best preserve color, flavor and medicinal potency.

To see if a flower or herb is completely dry, rub a piece between your fingers. It should feel crisp and crumble easily. If not, just dry a bit longer. Before storing, strip leaves and flowers from stems. The stems can be composted or bundled together and saved to use as fire starters in the winter. To preserve aromatic essential oils within the plant and to extend shelf life, don't crush or powder the herbs until right before you're ready to use them in a recipe or project.

Store in clean, dry glass jars in a cool area out of direct sunlight. The shelf life for most dried herbs and flowers is 6 months to a year. Some, such as dandelion flowers, will fade and lose their color sooner than that. When you spot a drab herb in your collection, it's a good sign that it's past its prime.

Many flowers, such as dandelions, violets and rose petals, freeze well when spread in a single layer in heavy-duty freezer bags for six to nine months. You can also make teas with fresh plants, then strain and freeze in ice cube trays. Once they're completely solid, pop out the cubes and store them in labeled freezer bags for up to one year.

Flowers and herbs can most often be used directly from the freezer in a recipe that requires fresh flowers. Once fully thawed, they'll be a little on the mushy side though. Teas can be thawed overnight in the refrigerator.

If you're not sure if your favorite herb or flower will freeze nicely, the best way to find out is to take a few leaves or petals, freeze them for one week, then see what the result is. In the majority of cases, the plant will freeze fine. In the worst case, you can compost the test result, but you'll still have learned something new!

Infusing Oils

By steeping herbs and flowers in oil, their beneficial properties can be harnessed for use in soaps, salves, lotions and other homemade products. Be sure the plant matter is dry before infusing. Water trapped in the oil can cause a cozy spot for bacteria and mold to grow.

There are three basic methods of infusing oil:

THE TRADITIONAL SLOW METHOD

This way requires the most patience and time, but results in a strongly infused and potent oil.

Fill a glass canning jar one-fourth to one-half of the way with dried herbs or flowers. Next, fill the jar, almost to the top, with your chosen oil. You have a wide variety of options when it comes to oils, although some of the most commonly used ones include olive, sunflower and sweet almond.

Cap the jar and tuck it away in a cool, dark cupboard for 4 to 6 weeks, shaking occasionally. A cool, dark area is suggested as too much exposure to heat and light may begin to degrade the quality of the herbs and oils during the extended length of the infusing time.

THE WARM SUNNY-WINDOW METHOD

This process gets a jump-start from the natural heat of sunshine and still results in a high-quality oil.

Fill a glass canning jar one-fourth to one-half of the way with dried herbs, then top off with oil just as you would for the traditional slow method. Secure a piece of cheesecloth or a coffee filter over the jar with a rubber band and place it in a warm, sunny window. This breathable layer allows for any potential condensation to escape, but will keep dust and flies from contaminating the oil.

Depending on how hot it gets, your oil may be sufficiently infused for use within 3 to 5 days. If you'd like to keep infusing past this time, to obtain a stronger oil, tuck it away in a cabinet for several more weeks. Short-term exposure to sunlight and heat is okay, but in the long term may cause the quality of the herbs and oils to degrade.

THE QUICK METHOD

This method works best if you don't have the time or desire to wait days or weeks to produce an infused oil. The finished oil might not always be quite as strong as the traditional slow-infused oil, but should still have noticeable benefits. Because it's solid at cooler room temperatures, coconut oil does best when infused this way.

Fill a glass canning jar one-fourth to one-half of the way with dried herbs or flowers. Next, fill the jar almost to the top with your chosen oil just as you would for the traditional slow method or warm sunny-window method above, but don't cap the jar. Instead, set the uncovered jar down in a saucepan containing a few inches of water, forming a makeshift double boiler of sorts. Place the pan over a low burner and heat for around 2 hours. Keep an eye on things while you do this to ensure that all of the water doesn't evaporate. If the water begins simmering or boiling, the heat is too high and should be turned down. You don't have to be precise, but try to keep the temperature somewhere around or less than 115°F (46°C) so you don't accidentally cook your herbs. After 2 hours have passed, remove the jar from the pan and set aside to cool.

You can also perform the quick method by infusing the herbs and oil directly in a slow cooker set to warm for 2 to 4 hours. Some slow cookers reach too high of a temperature to do this effectively, so you'll need to experiment with how your particular model works.

Once the oil has sufficiently infused via your preferred method, strain it through a fine mesh strainer or several layers of cheesecloth. Store the infused oil in a clean, dry jar in a dark, cool place, such as a cupboard. Sunlight and heat will shorten its shelf life, but when properly stored, infused oil should stay fresh for 9 months to a year.

Oils and Cosmetic Butters

There are a tremendous variety of oils and cosmetic butters available via the Internet and, increasingly, local stores as well. Sometimes, it's hard to choose which ones are the best to use.

When you first venture into making your own products, it's probably easiest to just grab some basic olive, sunflower and coconut oils from your local grocery or health food store. As long as they seem to have a fairly high turnover rate and the oils appear fresh, that's perfectly fine to do.

As you fine-tune your cosmetic-making skills, however, you may want to branch out into more exotic oils. For those, you can use one of the many vendors found online, some of which are listed in the resource section. Although it tends to appear more costly upfront because of shipping and buying in bulk, when you work out the price per ounce or gram, the ingredients obtained online are usually a better bargain and higher quality than grocery store oils.

The shelf life estimates of the oils and butters noted here are only guidelines and will vary widely depending on the quality and age of the oil when you buy it. Store in a cool area, away from direct heat and sunlight, and they may very well last even longer than listed.

Apricot Kernel Oil—a light yet nourishing oil that softens and moisturizes, and is suitable for all skin types. Apricot oil absorbs readily and helps relieve eczema and other itchy skin conditions. Shelf life is around 12 months.

Argan Oil—absorbs quickly and is wonderful for hair and nails. It improves and repairs skin, reduces the appearance of wrinkles and can be used in formulations to prevent stretch marks. It's expensive, so if it's out of your budget, try using sweet almond or another easily absorbed oil instead. It won't have the same array of benefits, but it will still produce a nice product. Shelf life is 18 to 24 months.

Avocado Oil—a rich oil, high in B vitamins and essential fatty acids. It does well in hair-care recipes and is useful for those with sensitive or irritated skin. Because it's pressed from the fruit, avocado oil is an excellent choice for those with tree-nut allergies. Shelf life is around 12 months.

Babassu Oil—a great substitute for those who are allergic to coconut oil. Babassu oil is moisturizing, slightly cooling and good for dry, damaged skin and hair. Shelf life is 18 to 24 months.

Castor Oil—a thick oil that lends a glossy shine to homemade lip balms, protects skin and has mild antifungal properties. Its low comedogenic status means it's unlikely to clog pores. In soap recipes, it helps boost lather. Shelf life is 24 to 36 months.

Cocoa Butter—rich and creamy, high in vitamin E and other antioxidants, helps soothe and protect skin. The unrefined version has a strong chocolate-like scent that carries through to the finished product. This works really well with some essential oils such as peppermint, but in other cases, you may wish to use a refined version so it doesn't overpower. Cocoa butter also adds hardness and a creamy lather to soap recipes. Shelf life is 24 to 30 months.

Coconut Oil—melts at 76°F (24°C), moisturizes and protects skin. Coconut oil is popular for use in hair masks and treatments, and its antibacterial properties make it a good addition to homemade deodorant recipes. In soap, it contributes to a hard bar and lots of lather. Some people experience redness and dry skin after using coconut oil for an extended period of time, and it has also been known to exacerbate acne. In that case, babassu oil makes a fine substitute in virtually all applications. Coconut oil is available in unrefined or refined form. Unrefined oil is suggested for use, as it may contain beneficial properties lost in the refinement process, but refined can be used equally as well if that's what you have available. For soap making, refined oil is often the better choice due to cost. Shelf life is 18 to 24 months.

Grapeseed Oil—a light oil that absorbs quickly, without leaving a greasy feeling. It's suitable for those with oily or acne-prone skin. Grapeseed oil also works well as a massage oil or blended with heavier oils to improve absorption. Shelf life is 6 to 9 months.

Hemp Seed Oil—a rich, nutritious oil that's excellent for skin and hair-care products. It's wonderful for dry, broken skin and is often used in formulations for eczema and psoriasis. The unrefined oil is a deep green color and should be kept in a very cool area or refrigerated when not in use. Sometimes, confusion exists about hemp seed oil and its connection to cannabis. The oil does not contain detectable levels of THC and is perfectly legal to use. Shelf life is around 12 months.

Jojoba Oil—a liquid plant wax that closely mirrors how our skin's sebum performs. Because of this, it's outstanding for hair, scalp and skin care. Jojoba is considered non-comedogenic, making it excellent for problem skin, while at the same time able to soften and soothe very dry skin. Jojoba oil is quite stable, with a shelf life of at least 3 to 5 years.

Kokum Butter—a hard and flaky cosmetic butter. Combine it with other oils and ingredients to help treat dry, cracked, inflamed or damaged skin. It also makes a good substitute for cocoa butter. Shelf life is 18 to 24 months.

Mango Butter—rich and creamy, moisturizes and softens skin. It can soften the appearance of wrinkles, so it is often used in antiaging products. It can usually be interchanged with shea butter in recipes. Shelf life is 18 to 24 months.

Meadowfoam Seed Oil—has a long shelf life and helps extend the shelf life of other, more fragile oils in a product in which it's included. Meadowfoam seed oil is moisturizing and softens hair and skin. It makes a good substitute for jojoba oil. Shelf life is 36 months.

Neem Oil—a strongly scented and powerful oil, used for treating skin conditions such as acne and psoriasis. It has antimicrobial, antiviral, antifungal and antiparasitic properties and repels lice, ticks, mosquitoes and other pests. Because of the strong smell, it's recommended to use neem in small amounts. If pregnant or nursing, consult with your midwife or health care provider before using neem-containing products. Shelf life is 18 to 24 months.

Olive Oil—a readily available oil that works well in most cosmetic recipes and with most skin types. In the supermarket, olive oil is available in grades ranging from dark green extra virgin to a more refined, light-colored oil. All types of olive oil will work for the recipes in this book. Be aware that many store-brand light olive oils are cut with canola oil to reduce costs and are often past their prime. They'll still work in your soap recipes, but your bars may yellow or go rancid sooner than if you purchased a higher-quality product from online shops that deal specifically in soap-making supplies. Shelf life is 12 months.

Rice Bran Oil—excellent for use in eye creams and serums, as it may help reduce the appearance of dark circles and under-eye puffiness. Rice bran is also a good choice for shampoo bars and hair-care recipes. Shelf life is around 12 months.

Rosehip Seed Oil—a premier antiaging oil that helps smooth the appearance of wrinkles, regenerates skin and reduces scars. It's light, nongreasy, absorbs quickly and doesn't leave your skin feeling oily. Rosehip seed oil should be stored in a cool location or your refrigerator. Shelf life is 6 to 12 months.

Sesame Seed Oil—a medium-weight oil that's high in vitamin E and may be useful for dry skin. Shelf life is 12 months.

Shea Butter—high in vitamins A and E, ideal for treating dry, weathered or damaged skin. Unrefined shea has a rather strong scent that some find unpleasant. If that's the case for you, look for a refined version that hasn't been processed with bleach or chemicals. Avoid extreme temperature fluctuations and overheating, or your shea butter may develop graininess. Shelf life is 12 to 18 months.

Sunflower Oil—a light, non-comedogenic oil that's high in lecithin and vitamins A, D and E. Sunflower is one of the best oils for applying to broken, damaged or aging skin. Shelf life is 9 to 12 months.

Sweet Almond Oil—suitable for most skin types. It's high in fatty acids, anti-inflammatory, softens skin and may help improve hair health and growth. It makes for a good massage or after-bath oil. Shelf life is around 12 months.

Tamanu Oil—a high-quality, unrefined tamanu oil has a distinct, deep scent. If you have tree-nut allergies, consult with your physician first to determine if you should use tamanu oil. It's remarkable for treating scars, sores, stretch marks and a variety of skin conditions. Its antibacterial properties make it a good addition to acne formulations, and with its anti-inflammatory traits, it's a nice addition to sore-muscle salves and balms. Shelf life is 12 to 18 months.

Additional Ingredients

While herbal-infused oils can be useful and wonderful all on their own, they can also be turned into salves, soaps, lotions, creams and much more. In order to do that, you'll need one or more of the additional items listed below. I try to source most of my ingredients from local grocery or health food stores, but some specialty items may need to be ordered online. See the Resources section (page 330) of this book for recommended vendors.

Alkanet Root Powder—a plant-derived dye that can be used to color homemade cosmetics. Depending on how much you use, you can obtain shades ranging from pale pink to ruby red. In soap, however, the high alkalinity causes alkanet root to turn purple instead. If you're pregnant, check with your midwife or doctor before using alkanet.

Aloe Vera Gel—a clear, thick gel extracted from the leaves of aloe plants. It's great for treating skin irritations, burns and bug bites. Look for aloe vera gel near the pharmacy or sun-care area of your local grocery or drugstore. You can also find it in most health food stores. Even the most natural brands will have some type of preservative, but avoid synthetically colored gel or those with a lot of additives. The recipes in this book were developed and tested using a thick gel. If your brand of aloe is water-like, you'll probably need to use less of it, and the end product may turn out differently.

Annatto Seed Powder—gives soaps and cosmetics a yellow to orange tint, depending on how much you use. It tends to work best when mixed with or infused in the oil portion of your recipe.

Arrowroot Powder—a white, lightweight starch that helps absorb excess oil in some recipes. Look for arrowroot powder or starch in the gluten-free baking section of your local supermarket or health food store. If you can't find any, you can use cornstarch for a similar action in many recipes.

Baking Soda—(also known as sodium bicarbonate) a common, natural baking ingredient. It helps soften water, making it a great addition to bath salts. Combine it with citric acid to make fizzing bath salts. Along with vinegar, it's commonly used as an inexpensive and nontoxic cleaning agent.

Beeswax—a faintly honey-scented yellow wax, produced by honeybees. It helps thicken creams and hold salves and lotion bars together. It has beneficial skin-softening properties and helps your skin retain moisture.

Candelilla Wax—a vegan alternative to beeswax, made from the leaves of a small shrub bearing the same name. You don't need as much candelilla to harden a recipe. Instead, use a little more than half as much as the amount of beeswax called for. For example, if a recipe calls for 5 grams of beeswax, try 3 grams of candelilla. Be aware that candelilla wax sometimes has a strong smell that carries through to the finished product. It also tends to make a shinier end product than beeswax.

Castile Soap—a mild and gentle all-purpose liquid soap that can be used in a variety of body, hair and cleaning recipes. You can find it in most health food stores and in many supermarkets.

Chlorella—a single-celled algae used as a nutritional supplement. For our purposes, it makes a great colorant to tint lip balm and soap a pale green.

Citric Acid—a natural crystalline powder that's derived from the fermentation of fruit sugars. Pair it with baking soda in bath salt recipes to make a fun, fizzy reaction when they meet together in the bathwater. Look for citric acid near the canning jars in local grocery or feed stores. You can also order it in bulk online for a much lower cost.

Clays—come in a variety of mineral-rich natural colors, including kaolin (white and rose), bentonite (gray), French (green), Cambrian (blue) and Brazilian (yellow, purple, red and pink). Clays draw out and absorb oils and dirt, making them great for use in face masks, body powders and deodorants. They're also excellent, long-lasting colorants in soap and some cosmetics.

Emulsifying Wax NF—makes lotion-making a breeze. Emulsifying wax can be sourced from plants, animals or petroleum, so read product descriptions carefully. The "NF" part means that it's National Formulary approved, or standardized, and is the type used to develop the recipes in this book. If you use a general emulsifying wax without the "NF" label, it may not work in quite the same way. See the Resources section (page 330) in the back of this book for a recommended supplier of vegetable-sourced emulsifying wax.

Epsom Salt—often used in baths to relieve sore and achy muscles or as a scrub for exfoliation purposes. There's also evidence suggesting that some of the magnesium and sulfate in Epsom salt is beneficially absorbed via the skin while bathing. Look for Epsom salt in the pharmacy section of your local grocery store.

Essential Oils—strong, concentrated extracts distilled from flowers, herbs and other plants. It takes a massive amount of plant material to produce just a tiny bit of essential oil. Because of this high cost in plant life, essential oils can be quite expensive. They're also deceptively powerful and can easily be overused. Essential oils are suggested in some recipes for fragrance or to complement a product's effect, but this book takes the position that employing the benefits of a whole plant is generally preferable to using an extract.

Honey—a wondrous product from the beehive! Its antibacterial nature makes it a strong ally when fighting wounds and other skin afflictions that just won't heal. It can be used directly, or infused with herbs, for a skin-softening face wash. Taken internally, it may help seasonal allergies, ulcers and a host of other minor ailments.

Neem Powder—derived from an evergreen tree, native to India. It's an effective pesticide and insect repellant. Pregnant women should not use neem without consulting their midwife or health care provider first.

Oats—soothe rashes and skin inflammation. Most grocery stores carry both regular rolled oats and certified gluten-free oats for those with sensitivities.

Sea Salt—can usually be found in the baking section of most grocery stores. It can be used in scrubs and bath soaks.

Stearic Acid—naturally derived from vegetable or animal fats, then further processed to make white waxy flakes that can be used to help thicken lotion and cream recipes. I find it especially helpful to stabilize creams made with beeswax but no emulsifier.

Sunflower Wax—another vegan option to use instead of beeswax. It has very firm holding power, which means you only need a fraction of it to replace beeswax in a recipe. It has no detectable odor and tends to leave finished projects a bright white unless tinted with a natural colorant.

Vegetable Glycerine—a clear, sweet liquid used to soften and moisturize skin. It's also useful for making alcohol-free herbal tinctures. A small amount can be added to toners to keep them from being too drying, but if you add too much, your end result may be sticky.

Vinegar—a common astringent and acidic liquid that can be used in hair and body care, home remedies and natural cleaning recipes. For skin, hair and health applications, use a high-quality apple cider vinegar. For household use, common plain white vinegar will be fine.

Washing Soda—made from sodium carbonate and can be found in the laundry section of many grocery stores. It's used in homemade laundry detergent recipes to more thoroughly clean clothes.

Witch Hazel—an anti-inflammatory and astringent that tones and tightens skin. It's particularly well suited to treating varicose veins, hemorrhoids, bruises and rashes, such as those caused by poison ivy. Look for witch hazel in the pharmacy section of your local grocery store, near the rubbing alcohol.

Substitution Tips

You'll get the best results from the recipes in this book if you follow the ingredient lists and directions carefully. Sometimes though, allergies, individual preferences or ingredient availability makes that impossible to do. At other times, you may want to put your own personal spin on a recipe and use it merely as a jumping-off point for a completely new creation you have in mind. While the following tips should help with substitutions, be aware that it may take several tries and some experimentation to get an adapted recipe to turn out right.

If a recipe calls for a type of oil that you don't have available, try substituting one with similar properties. For example, hemp seed oil is a rich, nutritious oil that's good for your skin. Avocado oil shares many of the same benefits and characteristics and will usually make a fine substitute for hemp. If you don't have either one available to you, though, perhaps try some olive oil instead. It might not always work in the exact same way, but almost any liquid oil can be substituted for another. If, for some reason, it doesn't work out, make a note of it and use your newfound knowledge to make an even better product the next time!

Shea and mango butter have a similar texture and usually can be interchanged. Kokum and cocoa butters are both very hard and often can be substituted for each other. You might not always need as much of a hard butter as you would a soft butter. So, if you have a recipe that calls for 50 grams of shea butter, you may only need 40 grams, or less, of cocoa butter to replace it. Start by adding a small amount and see how it does. You can always add more of something if needed.

Because coconut oil melts readily above 76°F (24°C) and instantly as it comes in contact with warm skin, I tend to categorize it with liquid oils. If you need to substitute something for it in soap, the best option is babassu oil. In lip balms, lotions and salves, use babassu or a liquid oil, such as sunflower or olive.

Vegans and those who need to avoid beeswax can substitute candelilla or sunflower wax instead. Keep in mind, however, that these are not direct one-to-one substitutions. It only takes a little more than half as much candelilla wax to firm and bind a product as it does beeswax. You need even less sunflower wax, about one-quarter as much. This is a rough formula to use as a starting guideline; individual recipes that you're converting will still need a bit of experimenting to get right:

10 GRAMS BEESWAX = 5 TO 7 GRAMS CANDELILLA WAX = 2 TO 4 GRAMS SUNFLOWER WAX

Ingredient quality, texture and other such properties tend to vary quite a bit between suppliers and even within batches of the same product. As you become more familiar with how an ingredient acts and feels in the recipes that you try, you'll build an inner awareness of when something needs adjusting, and will hopefully become more comfortable trying out bolder substitutions.

When it comes to plant availability, if you don't have a particular flower or herb needed for a body-care recipe, it can usually be interchanged, or in some cases, completely omitted. As when substituting oils, waxes and butters, the properties and appearance of the final product will be somewhat altered, but that's not usually a bad thing. The chances are high that you'll love your new creation!

In almost any body-care recipe, sunny yellow flowers such as dandelion, sunflower, calendula and chamomile can be swapped for one another. Lavender leaves make a great stand-in for rosemary; plantain leaves can be subbed out for violet leaves or chickweed. For the anti-acne products, thyme, sage, calendula and yarrow can be used interchangeably.

When making products for internal use, such as cough syrups and throat sprays, it's best to stick with the exact herbs called for in the recipe. Only use a substitution if it is recommended in the recipe notes.

You'll notice that I employ many herbal-infused oils in my projects. These enrich the products, making them more effective and tailored to treating certain conditions. If you can't find the herbs or flowers needed, or find that you're too pressed for time to make an infused oil, or perhaps don't have the space to store multiple jars of infused oils, then you can almost always use plain un-infused oil in place of an infused oil.

Preservatives, Antioxidants & Shelf Life

One of the great benefits of making your own natural care products is the ability to avoid synthetic ingredients and preservatives that are potentially harmful to your health. The tradeoff, of course, is that handmade products will not have the longevity that their store-bought counterparts do.

SHELF LIFE

The shelf life of the recipes in this book will vary widely, based on the freshness of the ingredients that you start with, the cleanliness of your equipment, how and where the product is stored and whether or not it contains water-based ingredients.

Items that have no water in them, such as lip balm, salves, balms, lotion bars, bath salts and bath scrubs will have a longer shelf life than lotions and creams containing water. Some oils, such as grapeseed, have a relatively short shelf life of six months. Any product containing that oil will have a shortened shelf life to match. Conversely, jojoba is very stable and can stay fresh for three to five years. Combined with just beeswax, it makes a product that could quite likely last for at least half a decade.

Generally, though, you can assume that lip balm, salves, lotion bars and so forth have an estimated shelf life of 6 to 9 months, or possibly longer. Storing your creations in direct sunlight or high heat will cause the quality to deteriorate much more quickly.

ANTIOXIDANTS

Oil-based products won't mold or grow bacteria, but they will turn rancid. You'll know they're well past that point when they start smelling unpleasant and like old oil. While you can add antioxidants to slow down rancidity, you won't be able to completely stop it. Two popular antioxidants include vitamin E and rosemary extract.

Vitamin E is fairly easy to find in gelcaps or liquid form. While it's also terrific for skin care and minimizing scars, try adding the contents of one gelcap or around 1 percent to lip balms and salves to help lengthen shelf life.

Rosemary Extract is a CO_2 extract of rosemary, not to be confused with the essential oil. It helps to protect oils from rancidity. You only need an amount as small as 0.1 percent of the recipe to be effective. To best protect its potency, don't melt it with waxes and butters; wait until hot mixtures have cooled slightly before adding. Rosemary extract also can be added to bottles of more fragile oils such as hemp, rosehip and grapeseed to help them last longer in storage.

While vitamin E and rosemary extract will help slow down oxidation of oils, they won't kill germs, so are not considered preservatives.

PRESERVATIVES

For years, I made our family lotions and creams with no preservatives because I thought all preservatives were bad for you. I later learned that there are safe, nature-derived preservative options available and several that are also approved for use in organic products!

While they're milder and don't have a shelf life comparable to store-bought lotions, they're perfectly sufficient for crafty types who make small batches, and use them up within a month or two. If you plan to sell products, they must be challenge tested and preserved; the recipes in this book were created for the home hobbyist.

PRESERVATIVES MENTIONED IN THIS BOOK

AMTicide® Coconut is a non-irritating anti-fungal that conditions skin. It's combined with natural preservatives, such as Leucidal® SF Max, to provide extra mold protection. It's created by fermenting coconut fruit with *Lactobacillus* and is Ecocert/COSMOS approved for organic products. Shelf life in lotions and creams is around two months if they're stored in a cool, dry place out of direct sunlight. Usage rate is between 2 and 4 percent of the recipe.

Leucidal SF Max is a salicylate-free antimicrobial that's derived from *Lactobacillus acidophilus*, a probiotic traditionally used to ferment yogurt. It is Ecocert/COSMOS approved for organic products. Combine it with AMTicide Coconut for better mold protection than if it's used alone. Shelf life in lotions and creams is around two months if they're stored in a cool, dry place out of direct sunlight. Usage rate is between 2 and 4 percent of the recipe.

Optiphen Plus is not considered all-natural, but is paraben-free and formaldehyde-free. It's considered one of the safer synthetic preservatives to use if you want your lotion to have a longer shelf life of six to nine months. Usage rate is 1 to 1.5 percent of the recipe. I use this preservative when gifting lotions and creams to family and friends.

HELPFUL TIPS FOR MAKING LOTIONS AND CREAMS

Water-based items, such as lotions and creams, can provide the right environment for mold and bacteria to grow. When making these, use the utmost care in keeping everything meticulously clean.

Sanitize your mixing utensils and jars by running them through your dishwasher if it has a sanitize cycle, or spray your equipment and containers with isopropyl rubbing alcohol and allow them to air-dry.

Distilled water is recommended because tap water can contain contaminants that might shorten shelf life. Herbal tea infusions can also shorten your lotion or cream's lifespan, which is why I usually recommend using herb- or flower-infused oil instead.

Use clean hands or gloves, and tie your hair back.

Consider using airless and pump-style bottles to store your lotions and creams. This keeps your fingers out of them, so they're less likely to get contaminated.

If you choose not to use a preservative in a handmade lotion or cream, or are too sensitive to use them, make a small batch at a time, store it in your refrigerator and use it up within one week.

Equipment You'll Need

You don't need a lot of fancy, costly equipment to get started making your own natural products. Much of what's required is probably already in your kitchen or can be found locally.

Hand Mixer—The lotions, creams and body butters in this book were developed using an inexpensive hand mixer. While you should be able to use a stand mixer just as well, you may end up with differing results if you use an immersion or standard blender.

Electric Coffee Grinder or Mortar and Pestle—For some recipes, dried herbs and flowers need to be powdered or coarsely ground. An inexpensive electric coffee grinder or the more traditional mortar and pestle will do the job nicely.

Fine Mesh Strainers—These are handy for sifting powdered herbs or straining infused oils and teas. I like to keep two on hand when making things, one for dry ingredients and one for liquids.

Glass Canning Jars—Canning jars are pretty much indispensable in my mind! They're tough, designed to withstand heat and have handy measurement markings on the side. The smallest 4-ounce (120-ml) jars are perfectly sized for storing lotions, salves and such. Half-pint (250-ml) and pint (500-ml) jars can be used for infusing oils, steeping teas and storing herbs.

Digital Scale—While you can measure ingredients by volume, it's not always as reliable as measuring by weight. For the most consistent results, a digital scale is recommended. You can find a good one for a reasonable price at your local big-box store, usually in the kitchen tools area. I realize that not everyone has the ability to buy one right away, so I've included some recipes that can be measured by volume as well as weight. If you plan on making soap, however, a digital scale is a requirement because the lye and oils must be measured precisely to ensure a balanced bar of soap.

Double Boiler or a Makeshift One—A double boiler, or makeshift substitute, is important to use when heating beeswax and other oils. It utilizes more of an indirect, gentle heat that's less likely to damage your ingredients or cause a fire hazard.

If you don't own a double boiler, though, don't rush out to buy one. You can create your own instead. To do so, place the contents you want to heat or melt in a canning jar or other heatproof container. An unlined empty soup or other tin can will work too and may be helpful if you're dealing with something particularly messy or hard to clean up. Set the jar or can down in a saucepan that has 1 to 2 inches (2.5 to 5 cm) of water in it. Place the pan over the burner and heat for the recommended time, or until your ingredients are sufficiently melted.

Mixing Bowl, Measuring Cups, Etc.—You'll also need a variety of mixing bowls, measuring utensils and things to stir with. While you could use the items you keep on hand for

regular baking and such, it's sometimes hard to clean out all of the wax residue or essential oil scents. I like to have one glass mixing bowl, a spatula and a set of measuring cups and spoons just for my projects. That way if I use a strong essential oil when mixing up a lotion one afternoon, I don't risk my mashed potatoes smelling like it at dinner that night!

Small Food Processor—I have a mini food processor that I got as a gift more than 16 years ago and in spite of constant use, it's still going strong. This handy tool is perfect for chopping fresh herbs and blending small amounts of ingredients together.

How to Make Blocks of Beeswax Easier to Use

While you can purchase convenient beeswax pastilles online, most local beeswax will come in a 1-pound (450-g) or other large-sized block form. If you've ever tried grating a block of beeswax, you know it can be quite the frustrating workout!

To make measuring it a lot easier, place the beeswax block in a large tin can or heatproof glass pitcher. A can will make cleanup a breeze because it's disposable, while the pitcher will have the convenience of a spout that will make pouring the wax much easier.

Set the can or pitcher down in a large pot that has several inches of water in the bottom. You don't want to melt beeswax over direct heat, as that's a fire hazard, which is why we do it indirectly with a makeshift double boiler.

Place the pan over a low burner and melt the beeswax. This will take a long time, possibly around an hour. Keep an eye on things and check frequently that the water doesn't evaporate.

While the beeswax is melting, spread out parchment paper over several cookie sheets. You can also use freezer paper, shiny side up. Make sure the pieces are pressed very flat or your melted dots of beeswax will puddle together.

Once melted, remove from heat and pour tiny beeswax drops over the parchment paper, then allow them to cool. They won't be perfectly sized like commercial pastilles, but they'll be much easier to use than a bulky block.

You may have to return your wax to the heat a few more times to get the entire block melted, so it's something of an exercise in patience, but you only have to do it once and you'll have enough little bits of beeswax to last a very long time!

How to Measure Beeswax by Volume

For best results, use a digital scale to weigh out the amount of beeswax needed in a recipe. If you don't have one available, however, you can still measure beeswax by volume fairly accurately, if you employ the following tips and guidelines.

Grated beeswax, small beeswax drops (from the previous section) or purchased beeswax pastilles should be tightly packed into the measuring spoon. For easy release, try spraying the spoon with a spritz of baking spray first. Press the beeswax so firmly that the small pieces stick together and mold themselves to the shape of the spoon. You should be able to remove the pressed beeswax in a single dome-shaped piece. Using this technique with a standard measuring tablespoon will yield approximately 10 grams of beeswax.

Another way to measure beeswax by volume is by melting the wax and pouring it into a standard measuring tablespoon. Beeswax measured in this manner will weigh approximately 12 grams.

Preparation Times

While some of the recipes in this book are fairly quick to make, others require some degree of preparation, time and patience. Herbs and flowers need hours, days or sometimes weeks to steep their beneficial properties into water, vinegars and oil.

It's much like baking. Sure, a boxed mix is quick and easy to throw together, but a cake that's made from scratch, with fresh, wholesome ingredients and lots of loving care, is infinitely better and well worth the extra time and effort.

This is a traditional part of hand-making products and should be embraced. Enjoy watching as each stage unfolds and your raw ingredients transform into something completely new and amazing. Whenever possible, let your children help and share in the wonder and sense of satisfaction that comes when you create something that is good and useful for you, your family and the environment!

Nontoxic Herbal Skin Care

By making your own skin care products, you avoid the sketchy ingredients often found in their store-bought counterparts. In this chapter, I'll show you how to turn your favorite flowers and herbs into gentle cleansers, toners and skin-soothing gels suitable for the most sensitive skin types.

If you struggle with acne, be sure to try out the Anti-Acne Herbal Tea recipe (page 47); it has been a lifesaver for my teenage daughter's skin! Or try one of the recipes featuring thyme, a powerful ally against acne-inducing bacteria.

Polish away grime and flaky skin with beautiful botanical-infused cleansing bars and cleansing grains, and then finish off with my all-time favorite Herb Garden Facial Oil (page 53). I love how soft and smooth it leaves my skin!

These straightforward recipes are easy to personalize using plants that are available in your area, and they make wonderful gifts for those you love!

Floral Cleansing Grains

These flower-packed cleansers gently exfoliate your skin, leaving it feeling soft and smooth. Cleansing grains can contain a wide variety of ingredients, from ground oats, nuts, seeds, rice, beans, powdered milk and clays, so there's a lot of room for creativity when making them. Besides using cleansing grains on your face, you can also incorporate them in bath soaks or oatmeal bath bombs, such as in the Calendula Oatmeal Bath Bombs on page 133.

YIELD: 2½ TO 3 TBSP (19 TO 27 G)

CALENDULA OATMEAL

An ultra-simple blend of oats and flowers; suitable for all skin types

2½ tbsp (18 g) rolled oats

1 tbsp (1 g) dried calendula flowers

YARROW & GREEN CLAY

Helpful for oily and acne-prone skin

2 tbsp (14 g) rolled oats

1 tbsp (2.5 g) dried yarrow

½ tbsp (8 g) French green clay

CHAMOMILE ROSE

Enriched with milk and suitable for more sensitive skin types

2 tbsp (14 g) rolled oats

½ tbsp (4 g) milk powder (cow, goat or coconut)

½ tbsp (0.5 g) dried rose petals

½ tbsp (0.5 g) dried chamomile

½ tsp rose clay

LAVENDER & BLUE CLAY

Gently polishes all skin types

2 tbsp (26 g) white or brown rice

½ tbsp (1 g) dried lavender

1 tsp dried cornflower, or use more lavender

¼ tsp Cambrian blue clay

Grind all of the ingredients together in a coffee grinder until finely powdered. Store in an airtight container to keep them fresh and dry.

To use, clean your face of any makeup or product. Splash your face with comfortably warm water to dampen your skin. Place 1 to 2 teaspoons (5 to 10 g) of cleansing grains in the palm of your hand and mix with warm water, or another liquid, such as coconut milk, aloe liquid, hydrosol, yogurt or witch hazel, to form a paste. Gently apply and rub over the skin on your face and throat. Rinse well with warm water and follow with a moisturizer, if desired. Cleansing grains can also be used as a face mask by leaving the mixture on your skin for 5 to 10 minutes before rinsing off.

Flower-Infused Clay Cleansing Bar

This soap-free cleanser is loaded with nourishing cocoa and shea butters, beneficial flowers and deeply cleansing clay, along with oats, that gently exfoliate and soften skin. For a hint of added color, try stirring in a small amount of French green, rose, blue Cambrian or purple Brazilian clay. Solid clay cleansing bars work on a similar principle to the oil-cleansing method, in which you use oil or oil-based products to remove dirt from your face. In the bar shown, I used dandelion-infused sunflower oil, dried calendula and chamomile flowers, along with yellow Brazilian clay. This recipe is incredibly adaptable, so feel free to swap out your favorite flowers in the recipe to create one-of-a-kind bars. Some suggestions include rose petals, calendula, cornflower, dandelion, chamomile, violet, sunflower and elderflowers.

YIELD: 1 (4-OUNCE [113-G]) BAR

3 tbsp (30 g) cocoa butter

1 tbsp (14 g) shea butter

1 tbsp (11 g) flower-infused oil, such as apricot kernel, jojoba, cucumber seed or grapeseed (see page 18 for how to infuse oil)

2½ tbsp (18 g) rolled oats

2 tbsp (1.5 to 2 g) dried flowers

¼ cup plus 3 tbsp (38 g) white kaolin clay

¼ tsp yellow, rose, purple or French green clay (optional)

Weigh the cocoa butter, shea butter and infused oil in a half-pint (250-ml) heatproof jar or container. Set the container down in a small saucepan containing 1 to 2 inches (2.5 to 5 cm) of water, then place the pan over a medium-low burner until the butters have melted.

While the butters are melting, grind the rolled oats and dried flowers together in a coffee grinder until finely powdered.

Remove the melted butter mixture from the heat. Stir in the ground oats, dried flowers, white kaolin clay and the small amount of colored clay, if using. Mix well, then spoon into a 4-ounce (113-g) individual silicone mold, rapping the mold against the surface of your work area several times as you fill, to help the product settle into the design better.

Place in the refrigerator for 2 to 3 hours until the bar is completely cool and solid. Remove from the refrigerator and store in a tin or jar in a dry, cool area.

To use, break off or cut a small chunk from the bar. Splash your face with comfortably warm water, then gently rub the piece of cleansing bar over your damp skin. It's normal for the piece of bar to disintegrate as you use it. Run very warm or hot water over a washcloth, then wring it out and immediately lay it over your face for a few moments to help soften the butters and oil. Remove the washcloth and use it, along with more warm water, to wash your face until it's clean. Your skin may feel sufficiently moisturized after using. If not, follow with a light moisturizer.

The shelf life of this cleansing bar is 3 months or more, as long as it stays dry. Don't allow the bar to get wet or the shelf life will be shortened.

Honey, Rose & Oat Face Cleanser

This soap-free cleanser features wrinkle-fighting rosehip seed oil, soothing rose petals and skin-regenerating honey, making it ideal for dry, damaged or aged skin. The ground oats act as a gentle exfoliator to slough away patches of dull flaky skin, leaving a soft, clean feeling behind as it washes away. Daily use will leave your skin feeling smooth and nourished.

YIELD: FILLS A 4-OUNCE (120-ML) JAR

2 tbsp (14 g) rolled oats

¼ cup (2 g) dried rose petals

¼ cup (60 ml) raw honey

1 tsp rosehip seed oil

Using an electric coffee grinder or mortar and pestle, coarsely grind the oats and dried rose petals. In a small bowl, combine them with the honey. Add the rosehip seed oil and stir until thoroughly mixed.

Use a clean spoon to scoop a small amount into the palm of your hand. Gently rub over your face and neck. Wash off with warm water and a washcloth. Rinse your skin well and gently pat dry.

This cleanser will stay fresh for 2 weeks, as long as you don't introduce water into it. Over time, the honey may settle into a separate layer. This is normal and just requires a quick stir before use. Store tightly sealed, away from heat and direct sunlight.

Variation: While rosehip seed oil is one of the antiaging stars in this cleanser, if it's out of your price range, try sweet almond, hemp or sunflower oil for their moisturizing benefits instead.

Chamomile Honey Face Wash

While it may sound a little strange and sticky at first, a daily face wash of pure raw honey, used in place of soap, is a wonderful way to balance, cleanse and repair all skin types. Adding nutrient-dense flowers and herbs to the mix makes it that much better! Chamomile was chosen for this recipe because of its anti-inflammatory and mild cortisone-like effect, making this face wash perfect for anyone with red, inflamed or irritated skin. Use once or twice daily to help calm and soothe sensitive skin.

YIELD: 1/4 CUP (60 ML)

1/8 cup (5 g) fresh chamomile flowers

1/4 cup (60 ml) raw honey

Place the chamomile flowers in a small glass jar. Pour the honey over the flowers and stir. Cap the jar and set aside for 1 to 2 weeks, to allow the properties of the flowers to infuse into the honey. In order to best preserve its raw benefits, don't use heat to try to speed up the process.

After sufficient time has passed, you can either strain the honey, which is a rather messy job, or just work around the flowers as you use it.

To use as a face wash, rub the infused honey over your face and neck. Allow it to sit on your skin for a minute or so if you'd like.

Take a washcloth and run it under very warm water. Place the cloth over your face for 15 to 20 seconds, to allow the heat to soften the honey. Using the washcloth, gently wipe the honey from your face, rinsing the cloth out as needed. Finish with a final splash of warm, clean water on your face. Follow with your favorite moisturizer, if desired.

Store the infused honey face wash in a cool, dark area. Check before each use, but as long as the flowers remain completely covered by honey, it should stay fresh for several months.

Variation: Other flowers that work well in this recipe include roses (for toning and easing redness), calendula (for all-around soothing) and violets (beneficial for complexions that tend to be dry).

Violet Flower Cleanser

Violets and their soothing, moisturizing properties take center stage in this recipe, ideal for sensitive complexions that might otherwise be irritated by standard soap-based cleaners. Aloe buffers and protects delicate skin while witch hazel gently removes dirt and other impurities, without stripping away much-needed moisture. Use once or twice per day for softer, cleaner skin.

YIELD: FILLS A 4-OUNCE (120-ML) BOTTLE

½ cup (6 g) loosely packed fresh or frozen violet flowers

½ cup (120 ml) boiling distilled water

2 tbsp (30 ml) aloe vera gel

3 tbsp (45 ml) witch hazel

FOR THE VIOLET-INFUSED WATER

Place the violet flowers in a heatproof jar or small bowl. Pour boiling water over them and let steep for around an hour. The water will turn a light shade of blue. For most of the recipes in this book, simmering water is used to make floral and herbal infusions, but in the case of violets, the color is released best with boiling water. Strain, squeezing the violets as you do, which will darken the water further. Set aside 3 tablespoons (45 ml) of violet-infused water. Any remaining violet water can be frozen in ice cube trays for future use.

FOR THE VIOLET FLOWER CLEANSER

Combine the reserved violet flower water with the aloe vera gel and witch hazel. The mixture will turn from blue to a pale purple at this point. Pour into a small glass bottle or jar. Shelf life is 5 to 7 days, when stored in the refrigerator.

To use, dampen a cotton ball with a small amount and gently rub over your face. Follow with a fresh water rinse and a light moisturizer, if desired.

Variation: Pansies, violas and Johnny-jump-ups are in the same family as violets and share similar benefits. They can be used as a replacement if violets are not available in your area.

Lavender Castile Soapy Facial Cleanser

This recipe combines the cleansing power of pure vegetable castile soap with the skin-soothing properties of lavender. Because castile can be slightly drying, this recipe is best suited for those with oily or combination skin types. Lavender-infused grapeseed oil adds a nongreasy way to offset the soap, while raw honey packs a potent punch against acne and other inflammatory skin conditions. Use nightly to wash away the day's grime and buildup. Follow with a very light moisturizer, such as Grapeseed & Thyme Lotion (page 116).

YIELD: 4 TO 5 USES

1 tbsp (15 ml) liquid castile soap

1 tsp raw honey

1 tsp lavender-infused grapeseed oil (see page 18 for how to infuse oil)

1 tbsp (15 ml) water

1 to 2 drops lavender essential oil, for scent (optional)

In a small bowl, stir together the soap, honey and infused oil. It's normal for the soap to turn a cloudy brown color because of the honey.

Pour in the water and gently stir, just until incorporated. Add the lavender essential oil and stir one final time.

This is a water-based product and the shelf life won't be very long. Store the soap in the refrigerator and use within 1 week.

To use, pour $\frac{1}{2}$ to 1 teaspoon of cleanser in the palm of your hand. Use your fingers to work up a lather, adding a bit more tap water if needed. Gently smooth the cleanser over your face and neck, avoiding the eye area. Rinse thoroughly with warm water and pat dry with a clean towel.

Variation: For an even stronger effect against acne, try using thyme-infused oil in this recipe instead. You could also substitute 1 drop of tea tree oil for the lavender essential oil.

Cool Mint Body Wash

This minty body wash is a refreshing treat after a long, hot summer day. Liquid castile soap gently cleanses away dirt and grime, while mint-infused witch hazel cools aloe-softened skin. A few drops of peppermint essential oil will energize and uplift your spirits while intensifying the overall cooling sensation, but if you have extremely sensitive skin, you may want to leave it out.

YIELD: ½ CUP (120 ML)

1 tbsp (1 g) loosely packed fresh mint leaves, chopped or torn

¼ cup (60 ml) witch hazel

2½ tbsp (38 ml) aloe vera gel

2½ tbsp (38 ml) liquid castile soap

Peppermint essential oil (optional)

FOR THE MINT-INFUSED WITCH HAZEL

Place the mint leaves in a small glass jar and pour the witch hazel over them. Cap the jar, shake well and tuck away in a cabinet for at least 2 to 3 days, or up to 2 weeks. Strain and set aside 2½ tablespoons (38 ml).

FOR THE BODY WASH

In a small bowl, combine the reserved mint-infused witch hazel and aloe vera gel. Mix well until the aloe is completely dissolved into the witch hazel. Add in the castile soap and essential oil, if using, and gently stir.

Pour the finished body wash into a bottle for use in the shower. While glass is nonreactive and preferred for storing most homemade products, it's safer to use plastic around tubs and showers.

To use, pour a small amount into the palm of your hand, then rub both hands together to form a light lather. You can also use this with a bath puff for even more bubbles and cleansing action. Rub over your body, rinse well and enjoy the fresh, clean feeling it leaves behind.

Forsythia Clear Skin Toner

The cheerful yellow flowers of the popular springtime shrub forsythia are said to possess acne-fighting and anti-inflammatory properties, making this toner a suitable treatment for skin that tends toward redness and breakouts. Witch hazel gently lifts away dirt and grime, while glycerin ensures your skin stays smooth and hydrated, without the need for additional oils. Use once or twice a day to help tame oily and acne-prone complexions.

YIELD: 4 OUNCES (120 ML)

½ cup (6 g) loosely packed fresh or frozen forsythia flowers

½ cup (120 ml) simmering hot water

¼ cup (60 ml) witch hazel

¼ tsp glycerine

Variation: Thyme is another acne-fighting powerhouse and can be used instead of forsythia flowers.

FOR THE FORSYTHIA-INFUSED WATER

Place the forsythia flowers in a heatproof mug or mixing bowl. Pour the simmering hot water over them. Steep for 10 to 20 minutes, or until the water has turned a light yellow color. Strain and set aside ¼ cup (60 ml).

FOR THE FORSYTHIA TONER

Combine the reserved forsythia-infused water with the witch hazel and glycerine. Stir well and pour into a small glass bottle or jar.

To use, dampen a fresh cotton ball with the toner and swipe over your face after washing. Follow with a light moisturizer, if desired.

Shelf life is 5 to 7 days, when stored in your refrigerator.

Anti-Acne Herbal Tea

This tea features the powerful combination of calendula, which calms troubled skin and promotes healing of scars, plus acne-busting thyme. Other skin-clearing herbs to consider incorporating into your tea include sage (drying and astringent), spilanthes (antimicrobial), purple coneflower (readily kills *P. acnes*, which is the main cause of acne vulgaris) and yarrow (astringent and anti-inflammatory).

YIELD: 1½ CUPS (375 ML)

½ cup (15 g) fresh or (8 g) dried calendula flowers

¼ cup (5 g) fresh or dried thyme

1½ cups (375 ml) simmering hot water

Place the calendula and thyme in a pint (500-ml) canning jar. Pour the simmering water into the jar and cover with a saucer. Steep for 2 to 3 hours. Strain and store in the refrigerator for up to 3 days.

For longer storage, pour in ice cube trays and freeze until solid. Store the frozen tea cubes in the freezer for 5 to 6 months. When you're ready to use one, thaw it in the refrigerator overnight, or gently melt it in a small saucepan over low heat.

To use, clean your skin of any makeup or product. Soak a cotton ball or corner of a washcloth with the tea and gently dab over your face, neck, chest, back or wherever acne plagues you. Leave the tea on your skin and allow it to air-dry. You may find it more effective to heat the tea to a comfortably warm temperature before applying, but it can also be applied cool or at room temperature. To be most effective, the tea should be applied once or twice daily.

Dandelion Thyme Vinegar Toner & Tonic

A tincture of dandelion is often prescribed as an internal remedy for acne. It works by improving digestion and boosting liver function. Thyme contains potent compounds that eliminate many types of bacteria, including the kind that causes acne. Together, the two herbs unite in this superpowered infusion that can be applied externally, and also taken by the spoonful to deliver a one-two punch to problem skin. A small amount of raw honey can be added for an extra antimicrobial boost and to soften skin in need of a bit of oil-free moisture.

YIELD: 1 ½ CUPS (375 ML) TONER

¼ cup (5 g) chopped fresh dandelion leaves, stems, roots and flowers

¼ cup (5 g) chopped fresh thyme leaves, stems and flowers

½ cup (120 ml) apple cider vinegar

1 to 2 tsp (5 to 10 ml) honey (optional)

½ to 1 cup (125 to 250 ml) water for dilution

Tip: If fresh herbs or flowers aren't available, use half as much dried instead.

FOR THE INFUSED VINEGAR

Place the chopped herbs in a small glass jar. Pour in the apple cider vinegar. If needed, add extra vinegar until the herbs are completely covered. Stir and cap with a plastic lid. If you only have metal lids, place a few sheets of wax paper or plastic wrap over the jar before sealing, to prevent the vinegar from corroding the metal.

Shake well and allow to infuse in a cool, dark place for 1 to 2 weeks. Strain. The shelf life of this vinegar is at least 1 year.

To use as a tonic, try mixing 1 teaspoon of infused vinegar with an equal part of raw honey and taking once daily. If you're pregnant, nursing or have medical conditions or concerns, check with your doctor before ingesting thyme-containing remedies like this one.

FOR THE VINEGAR TONER

Combine the infused vinegar with the water. Dilute the toner with enough water to make it comfortable when you rub it over your skin. If you have very sensitive skin, use the full amount of water. You may also want to add raw honey in the winter months, to prevent excess dryness. Shake well and label clearly. Store in a glass jar out of direct heat and sunlight. It should stay fresh and usable for several months.

To use, dampen a clean cotton ball with the diluted vinegar and rub over your face after washing. Allow to air-dry, then proceed with a light moisturizer, if desired.

Basil & Rose Kombucha Toner

Basil is a powerful herb with impressive anti-inflammatory effects and has also been studied for its role as an antiaging ingredient in cosmetic creams. In this recipe, it combines with cooling and skin-soothing rose. Kombucha, a fermented tea drink, may seem like an unusual ingredient for a toner, but has been shown to have benefits for your skin that are similar to apple cider vinegar. Some long-term users of kombucha-based toners have also reported noticeably younger, smoother-looking skin!

YIELD: 8 OUNCES (250 ML)

¼ cup (2 g) fresh or dried rose petals

¼ cup (2 g) fresh basil, torn

8 oz (250 ml) kombucha

Place the roses and basil in a glass canning jar and then pour in the kombucha.

Cap the jar and place it in the refrigerator to infuse for 3 or 4 days. Strain and return to the refrigerator for storage.

To use, apply the toner to a cotton ball and gently wipe over your face at night, after washing. Follow with a moisturizing cream or lotion.

Kombucha toner should be stored in a glass jar and will stay fresh for 2 weeks in your refrigerator. Discard if signs of mold appear.

Variation: Try using soothing chamomile or skin-regenerating calendula flowers instead of basil and roses.

Violet-Infused Aloe

Rub this soothing gel over mild irritations such as sunburn, bug bites, rashes, dry skin, razor burn and minor scrapes. The natural skin-calming and anti-inflammatory properties of aloe and violet, combined with its coolness from being stored in your refrigerator, will usually bring about rapid relief. Besides using straight from the jar, you can also incorporate it into creams or lotions, such as Violet & Aloe Moisturizing Cream (page 127).

YIELD: ½ CUP (120 ML)

½ cup (3 g) loosely packed fresh violet petals

½ cup (120 ml) bottled aloe vera gel

Place the flower petals and aloe vera gel in the bowl of a small food processor. Blend them together thoroughly. The mixture may get a little frothy in the process, but that's okay.

After blending, strain the now purple-colored aloe through a fine mesh sieve. You'll need to use your fingers to press and squeeze out most of it. The consistency of bottled aloe vera gel varies widely between brands; if yours is particularly difficult to strain, you may need to stir in a few drops of water to facilitate the process.

Store the finished violet-infused aloe in a glass jar in the refrigerator. It should stay fresh for several weeks or longer. For longer storage, freeze in ice cube trays and store individual cubes in freezer bags for 3 to 6 months. The frozen cubes can also be rubbed over sunburnt or irritated skin to cool and soothe away pain and inflammation.

➳ See picture on page 30.

Variation: Other flowers that work well in this recipe include chamomile, calendula and rose.

Herb Garden Facial Oil

Facial oils are lightweight and quick-absorbing skin treatments designed to nourish and help seal in moisture. They can be used alone or followed by your favorite moisturizer. Because of their richness, you only need a few drops for the oil to be effective! I designed this recipe with mature skin types in mind, but feel free to change up the herbs, flowers and oils in this recipe to best suit you. Rosehip seed oil is a premier product for fighting wrinkles, scars and weathered skin. If you struggle with breakouts, you may wish to use tamanu oil in its place. Grapeseed oil is super light, anti-inflammatory and absorbs quickly. Jojoba balances and leaves all skin types soft, and borage oil may help reduce the appearance of large pores. For a touch of added luxury and to boost the skin-repairing and antiaging effectiveness, I like to add a few drops of sea buckthorn oil, but it can be omitted if you wish.

YIELD: 3.4 OUNCES (100 ML) FACIAL OIL

¼ cup (8 to 12 g) dried crumbled herbs and flowers (see suggested list below)

¼ cup (60 ml) grapeseed oil

¼ cup (60 ml) sesame oil or more grapeseed oil

2 tbsp (30 ml) jojoba or argan oil

1 tbsp (15 ml) rosehip seed oil

1 tsp borage oil or more rosehip seed oil

2 to 3 drops sea buckthorn oil (optional)

Place the herbs and flowers, grapeseed oil, sesame oil and jojoba oil in a half-pint (250-ml) canning jar. Infuse the oil using one of the methods on page 18. Strain the finished oil into a new jar. Stir in the rosehip seed oil, borage oil and sea buckthorn oil, if using. Mix well and store in the refrigerator for up to 6 months.

To use, wash your face and leave slightly damp. Apply 3 to 10 drops to the palm of your hand and use your fingertips to gently smooth over your face and throat.

SUGGESTED HERBS AND FLOWERS

Thyme—anti-inflammatory, fights acne

Milk thistle—fights redness, may improve rosacea

Violet—soothing, great for dry skin

Rosemary—antioxidant rich

Calendula—regenerative, healing

Echinacea flowers—anti-inflammatory

Cooling Sunburn Cubes

Aloe vera is a well-loved remedy for sunburns, as it's highly effective at relieving the discomfort caused by too much time spent in the sun. In these sunburn cubes, aloe is combined with witch hazel, a powerful anti-inflammatory, along with fresh plantain and violet leaves, which offer soothing and cooling properties. Store these in your freezer and pull them out as needed to quickly relieve mild sunburns and other minor skin irritations such as razor burn, scrapes and itchy insect bites.

YIELD: 7 TO 8 CUBES

¼ cup (3 g) chopped fresh plantain leaves

¼ cup (3 g) chopped fresh violet leaves

½ cup (120 ml) witch hazel

½ cup (120 ml) water

¼ cup (60 ml) fresh or bottled aloe vera gel

Place the fresh plantain and violet leaves, witch hazel and water in a blender. Mix thoroughly until you create a thin plant juice or slurry. Strain the mixture through a fine mesh strainer into a clean jar.

Rinse the blender briefly with water to remove any stray bits of herb. Pour the strained plant juice back into the blender. Add the aloe and mix well.

Pour the mixture into ice cube trays and freeze until solid. Store the frozen cubes in airtight containers or bags in your freezer until needed, or for 6 to 9 months.

To use, remove a cube from the freezer and gently rub over sunburned or irritated skin. You can leave the herbal mixture on your skin, allowing it to air-dry, or you may wish to rinse it off with cool or tepid water.

Thyme & Raw Honey Mask

This mask is ideal for irritated or blemished skin. Thyme is a classic antibacterial and antiacne herb, and raw honey heals and soothes a variety of inflamed conditions. Tamanu is a well-researched and amazing oil that's been added to the recipe for its ability to repair damaged skin, scar tissue and a variety of other skin ailments. French green clay rounds out the mix and helps draw out impurities from within the skin. This mask will leave your skin feeling clean without stripping away moisture.

YIELD: 1 APPLICATION

1 tsp dried thyme leaves

½ tsp French green clay

½ to 1 tsp raw honey

¼ tsp tamanu oil

Using an electric coffee grinder or traditional mortar and pestle, grind the thyme leaves, then sift through a fine mesh strainer. This should yield around ½ teaspoon of thyme powder.

Stir the thyme powder and clay together in a small bowl, then stir in the honey and tamanu oil. If your skin is extremely oily, you may want to skip the oil and add more honey instead, if needed, until a thick paste is formed.

Using your fingers, generously spread the mask over your face and neck and leave on for 5 to 10 minutes. The honey makes the mask somewhat sticky, so it's okay if it doesn't go on perfectly smooth and even.

To remove, wet a washcloth in very hot, but still comfortable, water. Lay the cloth over your face and neck for around 30 seconds, then wipe the mask off. You may need to repeat this process a few times until the mask is no longer visible on your skin. Rinse off any remaining residue with clean running water.

Variation: If French green clay isn't available, try kaolin or another type of cosmetic clay instead.

Dried Flowers & Herbs Mask

Because of their ability to draw out dirt and deep-clean pores, cosmetic clays make terrific face masks. Try combining your favorite clay with ground flowers and herbs for an added boost of healing, soothing or bacteria-fighting properties. Below are a few recipes to get you started, but look at the list of flower and herb properties on pages 10 to 17 and get creative with what you have available!

To turn dry clay into a mask, you'll need to add enough liquid to it to form a paste that's easy to spread over your face. Those with dry or sensitive skin may choose to use moisturizing honey, milk or aloe, while someone with oily or acne-prone skin may use witch hazel.

Sage is a drying, antimicrobial herb, making the Sage Green Mask best suited for oily skin. Try mixing with witch hazel and apply to areas plagued with blackheads.

Inflammation-taming cornflower and soothing lavender pair up nicely in the pretty Lavender Blue Mask featuring Cambrian blue clay. This mask could be mixed with aloe for dry or combination skin or with witch hazel or water for oily complexions.

Powdered rose petals and pink kaolin clay make up the lovely Rose Pink Mask with astringent properties. Try mixing it with yogurt or milk to enjoy the benefits of their skin-softening alpha hydroxy acids.

YIELD: AROUND 2 TABLESPOONS (17 TO 20 G)

FOR THE SAGE GREEN MASK

1 tbsp (1 g) dried sage leaves

1 tbsp (16 g) French green clay

FOR THE LAVENDER BLUE MASK

1 tbsp (3 g) dried lavender flowers

1 tbsp (1 g) dried cornflower (bachelor button) petals

1 tbsp (16 g) Cambrian blue clay

FOR THE ROSE PINK MASK

1 tbsp (1 g) dried rose petals

1 tbsp (16 g) rose kaolin clay

Water, witch hazel, milk, yogurt or honey as needed to form a paste

Using a coffee grinder or mortar and pestle, grind the dried flowers and herbs to a fine powder, sifting through a fine mesh strainer if necessary. Stir the resulting powder into the clay until fully incorporated. Store in half-pint (250-ml) jars or containers. Shelf life is 1 year.

To use, place a pinch in the palm of your hand. Add a few drops of your chosen liquid until a paste is formed. Apply to your face and leave for 5 to 10 minutes, then rinse well with warm running water. Use once per week or spot treat problem areas as needed.

Naturally Soothing Salves & Balms

Salves and balms are soft, spreadable preparations for your skin consisting of herbal oils and beeswax. They can be applied to help heal, soothe or improve various skin and health maladies.

If you or someone you love suffers from arthritis or general aches and pains, try my family-favorite recipes, Cayenne & Ginger Arthritis Balm (page 74) and Muscle Aches Salve (page 66). While I designed Peppermint Pine Headache Salve (page 81) for headaches, it too can be used as a rub for mild muscle aches, especially those caused by tension.

Menthol Chest Balm (page 77) is an effective alternative to petroleum-based commercial products, and a must-have for my family's winter cold-care medicine cabinet.

As a former kid with severe eczema and lifelong sufferer of extra-dry skin, Chickweed & Violet Salve (page 65), along with Plantain & Yarrow Heel Balm (page 62) are personal favorites that I find myself reaching for frequently, especially when battling dryness caused by indoor heated air during winter months.

Once you've tried a recipe or two and seen how simple yet effective salves and balms are, check out the section on building your own salve (page 83) and share your new creations with friends and family!

Plantain & Yarrow Heel Balm

This creamy balm is especially suited for dry, rough heels. It can also be used to soothe other dry areas such as hands, knees and elbows. Yarrow offers antiseptic properties and is helpful for treating cracked, damaged skin, while plantain is a classic healing herb that is useful to repair and improve all sorts of skin afflictions. Tamanu is a powerful oil used to treat tough skin cases, such as eczema, psoriasis and scarring. It greatly contributes to the effectiveness of this recipe, but if you don't have any available, you can use more infused oil in its place.

YIELD: 2 OUNCES (60 ML)

1 cup (213 g) sunflower or sweet almond oil

¼ cup (11 g) dried yarrow

¼ cup (3 g) dried plantain leaves

½ tbsp (7 g) tamanu oil or more infused oil

½ tbsp (7 g) cocoa butter

1 tbsp (7 g) beeswax pastilles

⅛ tsp peppermint or lavender essential oil

3 drops tea tree essential oil

Infuse the sunflower oil with the yarrow and plantain, using one of the methods on page 18. Strain out and reserve ¼ cup (52 g) of the finished oil to use in this recipe.

In a half-pint (250-ml) canning jar or other heatproof container, combine the ¼ cup (52 g) of infused oil, tamanu oil, cocoa butter and beeswax. Set the container down in a small saucepan containing 1 to 2 inches (2.5 to 5 cm) of water, then place the pan over a medium-low burner until the cocoa butter and beeswax have melted.

Remove from heat and let cool for 5 minutes. Stir in the essential oils and place in the refrigerator for 10 to 15 minutes to cool, checking and stirring well every 5 minutes. Remove from the refrigerator and continue stirring every 5 to 10 minutes until a thick, creamy texture is achieved. Frequent stirring as the balm cools is key to creating a soft, spreadable texture.

Store the balm in a cool, dark area away from high heat and direct sunlight. Shelf life is at least 6 to 9 months.

To use, generously rub over your heels and feet before bed, then cover with a pair of socks. After several days of use, you should wake up with noticeably softer feet!

Chickweed & Violet Salve

This salve was specifically designed for those with dry, itchy skin and eczema. Chickweed is an anti-inflammatory that helps relieve rashes and eczema, while violet leaves skin cool and soothes redness and irritation. For specialty oils, I sometimes add tamanu oil to this recipe; other times I use baobab oil, which is exceptional at repairing damaged skin. Sometimes I can't choose between the two, so I double the recipe and use 1 tablespoon (14 g) of each. Both are equally good choices to use in this recipe, but if you're allergic to tree nuts, just use more infused oil instead.

YIELD: 2 (2-OUNCE [60-ML]) TINS

1 cup (213 g) sunflower oil

¼ cup (3 g) dried chickweed

¼ cup (3 g) dried violet leaves

1 tbsp (14 g) tamanu or baobab oil, or more infused oil

2 tbsp (14 g) beeswax pastilles

Infuse the sunflower oil with the chickweed and violet leaves, using one of the methods on page 18. Strain out and reserve ½ cup (104 g) of the finished oil to use in this recipe. If you'd like, you can replace the amount of used oil from the infusing jar with fresh sunflower oil to continue the infusion for future projects.

Place the ½ cup (104 g) of infused oil, tamanu oil and beeswax in a half-pint (250-ml) canning jar or heatproof container. Set the jar down in a small saucepan containing 1 to 2 inches (2.5 to 5 cm) of water, then place the pan over a medium-low burner until the beeswax has melted.

Remove from heat and carefully pour into tins or glass jars. The shelf life is at least 6 to 9 months, if stored in a cool location, out of direct sunlight.

Muscle Aches Salve

This is a variation of my family's favorite salve for aches and pains. My original recipe also includes infusing the oil with myrrh, frankincense, Saint John's wort, cayenne and yarrow, in addition to the herbs listed below, so feel free to adjust the recipe to include those or other herbs in the mix as well. The ingredient that makes this salve extra special is CBD oil; I use the same liquid hemp supplement that I take daily for its health benefits. If you use and are a fan of CBD oil, then I highly recommend adding it into this recipe. If not, it could be substituted with another powerful oil that's helpful for relieving pain, such as Saint John's wort oil or more tamanu oil. I use mango butter in this recipe for its anti-inflammatory properties, and also include a small amount of emulsifying wax for improved texture and to make washing up easier.

YIELD: 4 OUNCES (120 ML)

1 tbsp (1 g) dried arnica flowers

1 tbsp (9.5 g) dried comfrey root

1 tbsp (1 g) dandelion or goldenrod flowers

1.7 oz (48 g) sweet almond or sunflower oil

1.5 oz (43 g) grapeseed, safflower or rice bran oil

0.1 oz (3 g) castor oil

0.5 oz (14 g) beeswax

0.07 oz (2 g) emulsifying wax (optional)

0.14 oz (4 g) tamanu oil

0.25 oz (7 g) mango butter

0.25 oz (7 g) CBD oil (optional)

40 to 50 drops peppermint essential oil

30 to 40 drops lavender essential oil

8 drops rosemary essential oil, or 3 drops white camphor essential oil (optional)

Place the herbs and flowers, sweet almond oil, grapeseed oil and castor oil in a half-pint (250-ml) canning jar. Infuse the oil using one of the methods on page 18. Strain the finished oil into a new heatproof jar for making the balm.

Add the beeswax, emulsifying wax (if using), tamanu oil and mango butter to the jar of infused oil. Set the container down in a small saucepan containing 2 to 3 inches (5 to 7.5 cm) of water, then place the pan over a medium-low burner until the beeswax and butter have melted.

Remove from heat and let cool for 5 minutes. Stir in the CBD oil, if using, and the essential oils. Keep the salve in the jar you used to make it in, or spoon it into two 2-ounce (60-ml) glass jars or tins. Shelf life is at least 6 to 9 months if stored in a cool location, out of direct sunlight.

Please check local laws for your state before purchasing or using CBD oil. This salve is not intended for use by children.

Lavender, Coconut & Honey Balm

The raw honey in this balm is a wonderful skin-regenerating agent, making it perfect for rubbing over rough, dry areas such as elbows, knees and feet. Coconut oil helps moisturize and protect skin while lavender adds a sweet scent and calming element. This balm might be slightly sticky when you first apply it and takes a bit of time to fully absorb, so apply a thin layer before bedtime and enjoy waking up to noticeably smoother, silkier skin!

YIELD: ½ CUP (120 ML)

¼ cup (9 g) dried lavender flowers

½ cup (100 g) coconut oil

2 tbsp (20 g) tightly packed beeswax, grated or pastilles

1 tsp raw honey

Lavender essential oil (optional)

Infuse the lavender in the coconut oil using the quick method on page 19. Once it has sufficiently infused, strain the oil. You can store this infused oil for 9 to 12 months before making the balm, if you'd like.

When you're ready to make the balm, combine the lavender-infused oil and beeswax in a heatproof container such as a canning jar. For easy cleanup, you can repurpose an empty tin can for this project. Set the jar down in a small saucepan containing a few inches of water, then place the pan over a medium-low burner until the beeswax has melted.

Remove from heat and stir in the honey for 3 to 4 minutes. Allow the balm to thicken, undisturbed, for 5 to 10 minutes, then stir thoroughly for several more minutes. This extra amount of stirring will help prevent the honey from separating out of the balm.

If desired, add a few drops of lavender essential oil for scent, then spoon the finished balm into a glass jar. Massage into dry areas before bedtime and wake up to softer, smoother skin.

Shelf life of the salve is 6 to 9 months, if stored in a cool location, out of direct sunlight.

Variation: Not a fan of lavender? Try using chamomile or calendula for their skin-soothing properties. If you're allergic to coconut, try using another oil such as sunflower, avocado or sweet almond instead.

Sunflower Salve

When drying sunflowers for seed, don't forget to save the beautiful yellow petals for projects such as this one! The sunny flowers are skin soothing and anti-inflammatory. Paired here with sunflower oil, which has been shown to be especially effective at healing broken or damaged skin, this double sunflower combo is perfect for smoothing over areas of dry, chapped skin.

YIELD: FILLS 3 (2-OUNCE [60-ML]) TINS

¼ cup (5 g) dried sunflower petals

Around ½ cup (120 ml) sunflower oil

1½ tbsp (15 g) tightly packed beeswax, grated or pastilles

Lemongrass or sweet orange essential oil (optional)

Infuse the sunflower petals in the sunflower oil using one of the methods on page 18. Once it has sufficiently infused, strain the oil. You can store this infused oil up to 9 to 12 months before making the salve.

When you're ready to make the salve, measure or weigh the sunflower-infused oil and make sure you have ½ cup (120 ml). If needed, add a little more plain sunflower oil to reach that total. Place the infused oil and beeswax in a heatproof jar or container. Set the jar down in a small saucepan containing 1 to 2 inches (2.5 to 5 cm) of water, then place the pan over a medium-low burner until the beeswax has melted.

Remove from heat. If you'd like, add 4 to 5 drops of essential oil for scent at this time. Lemongrass and sweet orange are two choices that match the bright and sunny nature of this salve perfectly.

Carefully pour into tins or jars. Shelf life is 6 to 9 months, if stored in a cool location, out of direct sunlight.

Variation: Instead of sunflowers, you could also try sunny calendula, another wonderful skin-healing flower.

Regenerating Rose Balm

This soft balm harnesses the skin-calming properties of rose petals and the reparative action of rosehip seed oil. Shea butter is high in vitamins A and E and excellent for treating weathered or damaged skin, while sweet almond oil provides beneficial fatty acids and helps soften skin. At bedtime, dab this balm around your eyes, on laugh lines, your forehead and anywhere else you'd like to reduce the appearance of wrinkles, aging or scars.

YIELD: FILLS 3 (2-OUNCE [60-ML]) TINS

2 tbsp (1 g) dried rose petals, crumbled

Around ¼ cup (60 ml) sweet almond oil

¼ cup (55 g) shea butter

1½ tbsp (15 g) tightly packed beeswax, grated or pastilles

1 tbsp (15 ml) rosehip seed oil

Geranium or rose essential oil (optional)

Infuse the rose petals in the sweet almond oil using one of the methods on page 18. Once it has sufficiently infused, strain the oil. You can store the finished infused oil for several months before making the balm.

When you're ready to make the balm, combine the rose-infused oil, shea butter and beeswax in a canning jar or other heatproof container. Because rosehip seed oil is heat sensitive, we'll add that later. Set the jar down in a small saucepan filled with 1 to 2 inches (2.5 to 5 cm) of water, then place the pan over a medium-low burner until the beeswax has melted.

Remove from heat and let cool slightly. Stir in the rosehip seed oil. You can add 4 to 5 drops of geranium or rose essential oil at this time for scent or leave it unscented.

Carefully pour into 3 (2-ounce [60-ml]) tins or a small 4-ounce (120-ml) canning jar. Shelf life of the salve is 6 to 9 months, if stored in a cool location, out of direct sunlight.

Cayenne & Ginger Arthritis Balm

This balm is helpful for arthritis and other painful joint conditions. Cayenne peppers contain a beneficial compound called capsaicin, which has been shown to offer relief from arthritic and other types of pain. Ginger is traditionally used to increase circulation and to relieve pain when applied topically. Arnica flowers round out this powerful trio of herbs, and are helpful for swelling, bruising and arthritic joints. White camphor essential oil is used to relieve aches and pains, while lavender helps ease muscle tension. If white camphor isn't available, rosemary can be used as a mild analgesic in its place. Other essential oil options for pain relief include cypress, cedarwood or Himalayan or fir needle, any of which can be used to replace the lavender.

YIELD: 2 OUNCES (60 ML)

1 cup (213 g) rice bran or sunflower oil

¼ cup (5 g) chopped dried cayenne peppers

¼ cup (4 g) dried arnica flowers

¼ tsp ground ginger

2½ tsp (7.5 g) beeswax pastilles

1 tbsp (15 g) mango or shea butter

6 drops white camphor or rosemary essential oil

12 drops lavender essential oil

Infuse the rice bran oil with the peppers, arnica flowers and ground ginger, using one of the methods on page 18. Strain out and reserve ¼ cup (52 g) of the finished oil to use in this recipe.

In a half-pint (250-ml) canning jar or other heatproof container, combine the ¼ cup (52 g) of infused oil, beeswax and mango butter. Set the container down in a small saucepan containing 1 to 2 inches (2.5 to 5 cm) of water, then place the pan over a medium-low burner until the beeswax and butter have melted.

Remove from heat and let cool for 5 minutes. Stir in the essential oils and place in the refrigerator for 10 to 15 minutes to cool, checking and stirring well every 5 minutes. Remove from the refrigerator and continue stirring every 5 to 10 minutes until a thick, creamy texture is achieved. Frequent stirring as the balm cools is key to creating a soft, spreadable texture.

Shelf life is at least 6 to 9 months if stored in a cool location, out of direct sunlight. To use, rub over your aching joints and muscles. Avoid using on broken skin, and be careful not to rub your eyes after applying the balm.

Menthol Chest Balm

Skip the petroleum-based cold-care rub and try this all-natural version instead. Menthol crystals, naturally derived from mint oils, provide powerful cough relief and are boosted by a trio of eucalyptus, peppermint and white camphor essential oils, which add an extra layer of effectiveness by suppressing coughs while loosening congestion. Bee balm— or thyme-infused oil adds a touch of antiseptic and anti-inflammatory properties, but you could use plain oil instead and still have an effective product.

YIELD: 2 OUNCES (60 ML)

1 cup (213 g) sunflower or sweet almond oil

¼ cup (2 g) dried bee balm or thyme

2 tbsp (14 g) beeswax pastilles

¾ tsp (2 g) menthol crystals

17 drops eucalyptus essential oil

10 drops peppermint essential oil

3 drops white camphor essential oil

This rub was not designed for children under the age of ten years old.

Infuse the sunflower oil with the bee balm or thyme, using one of the methods on page 18. Strain out and reserve ½ cup (104 g) of the finished oil to use in this recipe. You can replace the amount of used oil from the infusing jar with fresh sunflower oil to continue the infusion for future projects.

In a half-pint (250-ml) canning jar or other heatproof container, combine the ½ cup (104 g) of infused oil and beeswax. Set the container down in a small saucepan containing 1 to 2 inches (2.5 to 5 cm) of water, then place the pan over a medium-low burner until the beeswax has melted.

Remove from heat and stir in the menthol crystals. Be aware that there will be momentary strong fumes when you do so. Stir in the essential oils and place the mixture in the refrigerator for 10 to 15 minutes to cool, checking and stirring well every 5 minutes. Remove from the refrigerator and continue stirring every 5 to 10 minutes until a thick, creamy texture is achieved. Frequent stirring as the balm cools is key to creating a soft, spreadable texture.

Shelf life is at least 6 to 9 months if stored in a cool location, out of direct sunlight. To use, rub a thin layer over your chest and throat. Avoid getting it in your eyes or other sensitive areas.

Charcoal Drawing Balm

This versatile balm is the perfect addition to your herbal first aid kit. Charcoal, clay and castor oil work in synergy to draw out boils, splinters and other foreign bits from under the skin. It's also an excellent remedy for insect bites, bee stings, infected ingrown nails and blackheads. Lavender essential oil benefits a multitude of skin conditions, while tea tree oil is a powerful antiseptic.

YIELD: 2 OUNCES (60 ML)

2 tbsp (21 g) plantain or calendula-infused sunflower oil (see page 18 for how to infuse oil), or other oil such as olive oil

2 tbsp (21 g) castor oil

½ tbsp (5 g) packed beeswax pastilles

½ tbsp (2.5 g) activated charcoal

½ tbsp (4 g) bentonite or kaolin clay

18 drops lavender essential oil

10 drops tea tree essential oil

In a half-pint (250-ml) canning jar or other heatproof container, combine the infused oil, castor oil and beeswax. Set the container down in a small saucepan containing 1 to 2 inches (2.5 to 5 cm) of water, then place the pan over a medium-low burner until the beeswax has melted, 30 to 40 minutes.

Remove from heat and stir in the charcoal and clay. Let cool for 5 minutes. Stir in the essential oils and place the balm in the refrigerator for 10 to 15 minutes to cool, checking and stirring well every 5 minutes. Frequent stirring as the balm cools is key to creating a soft, spreadable texture.

Keep the balm in the jar you used to make it in, or spoon it into a 2-ounce (60-ml) glass jar. Cover with a lid or top and store in a cool spot out of direct sunlight. Shelf life is 1 year or more.

To use, apply a tiny dab to the offending spot and cover with a Band-Aid. Leave it on at least overnight or all day. Remove the Band-Aid while bathing or showering, wash the area with mild soap and water, then reapply the balm if needed. Improvement may happen within a day, or it may take up to a week.

Tip: Charcoal balm could stain clothing and light-colored bedding, so keep it covered with a Band-Aid and be aware of its staining potential when using.

Peppermint Pine Headache Salve

This salve contains mint to cool inflammation and pine for its mild pain-relieving properties. Tamanu oil is a wonderful addition to pain-relief salves, but if you don't have any, just use more infused oil instead. While the mint-infused oil will have a faint scent of its own, peppermint essential oil adds a deeper cooling sensation that really helps make this salve more effective. Massage the salve onto your temples, forehead, back of neck and between your shoulder blades when suffering from a headache. Close your eyes, breathe deeply and consciously allow the muscles of your face, jaw and shoulders to relax.

YIELD: 4 OUNCES (120 ML)

2 tbsp (2 g) dried mint leaves, crumbled

2 tbsp (2 g) dried pine needles, chopped

²/₃ cup (160 ml) sunflower or olive oil

1 tbsp (15 ml) tamanu oil

0.5 oz (14 g) beeswax

¹/₂ to ³/₄ tsp peppermint essential oil

Infuse the mint leaves and pine needles in the sunflower or olive oil using one of the methods on page 18. Once it has sufficiently infused, strain the oil. You can store this infused oil for up to 9 to 12 months before making the salve.

When you're ready to make the salve, combine ¹/₂ cup (120 ml) of the infused oil with the tamanu oil and beeswax in a canning jar or other heatproof container. Set the container down in a small saucepan containing 1 to 2 inches (2.5 to 5 cm) of water, then place the pan over a medium-low burner until the beeswax has melted.

Remove from heat and stir in the peppermint oil. Carefully pour the hot mixture into tins or jars.

Depending on your preference, you may want a softer or firmer salve. If so, just remelt the product and add a pinch more beeswax for a firmer consistency or a little more oil for a softer salve.

If your pain persists, is chronic or gets worse, check with your health care provider for further advice.

Shelf life of the salve is 6 to 9 months, if stored in a cool location, out of direct sunlight.

Tip: Gather pine needles from the trees around your house and spread them out on a clean dishtowel for a day or two to dry. If you don't have pine trees in your area, try using a few drops of fir needle essential oil in your salve instead.

Exotic Body Butters & Lotion Bars

Body butters and lotion bars are super simple to whip up and make wonderful gifts for friends and family!

Lotion bars are something like a salve or waterless lotion, only in a more solid form. They're perfect for rubbing over dry hands, elbows, feet and heels. If you work outdoors or with your hands a lot, you'll find that lotion bars are one of the best treatments around for healing cracked, damaged skin.

While body butters share a similar ingredient profile with lotion bars, along with the same ability to nourish your skin, they have a light and fluffy consistency instead. They work well when applied after an evening bath or shower, and help to seal moisture in your skin all night.

Besides sharing several of my favorite body butter recipes in this chapter, I've provided a simple formula you can use over and over to design one-of-a-kind body butters, uniquely customized for your skin type and scent preferences (page 98). One of the best features about body butter is that it's waterless, so you never have to worry about preservatives or mold. Make, use and gift your creations freely!

Triple Sunshine Body Butter

Light and airy, this body butter feels like a dream on your skin! It's scented with an essential oil blend reminiscent of mock orange blossoms, and it features a trio of golden flowers that soothe and nourish as they add a soft yellow color to the finished product. Avocado butter absorbs quickly into the surface of all skin types, without leaving a greasy residue behind. If you don't have any available, try using shea butter in its place for a richer texture that stays on your skin longer. I chose apricot kernel oil for the batch shown because it's helpful for aged or itchy skin types. Other light oils that could work well in its place include grapeseed, hazelnut, jojoba, rice bran or borage seed oil.

YIELD: FILLS 4 (4-OUNCE [120-ML]) JARS

¼ cup (3 g) mixture of dried dandelion, chamomile and calendula flowers

1 cup (170 g) avocado butter

2 tbsp (17 g) refined cocoa butter

½ tbsp (7 g) apricot kernel oil or oil of choice

45 drops sweet orange essential oil

9 drops ylang-ylang essential oil

In a wide-mouth pint (500-ml) heatproof jar, combine the dried flowers, avocado butter, cocoa butter and apricot kernel oil. Place the jar in a saucepan containing a few inches (at least 5 cm) of water, forming a makeshift double boiler. Heat over very low heat for 30 to 45 minutes, stirring occasionally. Remove the container from the heat and strain into a 4-cup (1-L) glass measuring container or other tall narrow container, to make whipping the butter easier. Chill the infused mixture in the refrigerator for 30 to 35 minutes until it starts solidifying.

Remove the hardened butter from the refrigerator and whip with a hand mixer on medium-high to high speed until the texture is light and fluffy. If it seems too soft to hold a peak, put the container back in the refrigerator for another 5 or 10 minutes, then try whipping again.

Add the essential oils and beat the mixture for another 30 seconds, or until completely incorporated. Spoon the butter into jars and cover with their tops. Store in a cool, dry place out of direct sunlight. Shelf life is 6 months or more.

Bee Balm Intensive Hand Butter

Smooth this rich butter over dry hands at night and wake up to softer skin. Shea butter protects and heals chapped, cracked skin, while bee balm—infused sunflower oil improves your skin's barrier function and heals damaged skin. Fractionated coconut oil absorbs rapidly, making the overall product feel lighter and less greasy; if you're allergic to coconut or don't have any available, you can use more infused oil instead. Rosehip seed oil is exceptional for healing damaged skin and preventing signs of aging. The butter is scented lightly with bergamot essential oil.

YIELD: FILLS 4 (4-OUNCE [120-ML]) JARS

2 tbsp (23 g) bee balm—infused sunflower or sweet almond oil (see page 18 for how to infuse oil)

1 tbsp (12 g) fractionated coconut oil or more infused oil

3/4 cup (165 g) shea butter

1 tbsp (12 g) rosehip seed oil

30 to 40 drops bergapten-free bergamot essential oil (see tip)

In a wide-mouth pint (500-ml) heatproof jar, combine the infused oil, fractionated coconut oil and shea butter. The jar is perfectly sized to melt and mix the contents in the same container by using one beater attached to a hand mixer. Place the jar in a saucepan containing a few inches (at least 5 cm) of water, forming a makeshift double boiler. Heat over very low heat, just until the butter is melted.

Remove the container from the heat and let cool for about 3 minutes. Stir in the rosehip seed oil. Chill the mixture in the refrigerator for 30 to 35 minutes, or until it starts solidifying.

Using one beater in a hand mixer, whip on medium-high to high speed until the texture is light and fluffy. If it seems too soft to hold a peak, put the container back in the refrigerator for another 5 to 10 minutes, then try whipping again.

Add the essential oil and beat the mixture for another 30 seconds, or until completely incorporated. Store the butter in the jar used for mixing, or spoon into smaller jars and cover with their tops. Store in a cool, dry place out of direct sunlight. Shelf life is 6 months or more.

To use, rinse your hands with comfortably warm water and gently pat dry, leaving the skin slightly damp. Rub a small amount of butter onto your skin, where it will seal in the moisture. You could also use this on other dry spots such as knees, elbows and feet.

Tip: Bergamot essential oil contains bergapten and furanocoumarin compounds. They are phototoxic and make your skin likely to burn in the sun. Instead, look for bergamot essential oil that is labeled bergapten-free, furanocoumarin-free bergamot or bergamot FCF.

Dandelion Body Butter

Apply a thin layer of this airy body butter at night for smoother skin in the morning. Body butters are rich, so remember that a little bit goes a long way! Dandelion flowers were chosen for this recipe as they're especially effective at relieving chapped, dry skin. Mango butter softens and helps skin retain moisture, but if it's not available, shea butter makes an equally lovely stand-in. Sweet almond oil is high in healthy fatty acids and absorbs into your skin nicely, but if you're allergic to tree nuts, grapeseed is another excellent choice. Two popular essential oil choices for a clean citrus scent are litsea cubeba or lemongrass, but feel free to use your own personal favorite or omit altogether.

YIELD: FILLS 3 (2-OUNCE [60-ML]) JARS

2 oz (56 g) mango butter

1 oz (30 g) dandelion-infused sweet almond oil (see page 18 for how to infuse oil)

20 to 30 drops essential oil, for scent (optional)

1/8 to 1/4 tsp arrowroot powder (optional)

Place the mango butter in a heatproof jar or container. Set the jar down into a saucepan containing a few inches (at least 5 cm) of water. Place the pan over a medium-low burner just until the mango butter melts. Overheating the mango butter may cause graininess, so remove it promptly once melted. Stir in the dandelion-infused oil.

Pour the melted butter and oil into a small mixing bowl and place it in the refrigerator for about 30 minutes, or until it starts to firm up. Using a handheld mixer, beat for several minutes until light and fluffy, stopping to scrape the sides of the bowl several times.

Add the essential oil and arrowroot powder, then beat for another minute. Arrowroot or cornstarch are sometimes added to body butters to help cut some of the oily feel they have, but it's completely optional and okay to leave out if you don't have any or prefer not to use it.

Store the finished butter in a cool, dark area away from high heat and direct sunlight. Shelf life should be around 6 months.

Tip: During warm weather, you may want to slightly increase the mango butter or add a small amount of a harder butter, such as cocoa or kokum, so that the body butter won't melt. During cool weather, increase the amount of oil a bit, so that the body butter isn't too stiff.

Mint Cocoa Body Butter

Use a high-quality unrefined cocoa butter to create this deliciously decadent body butter that smells just like a peppermint patty! In this recipe, I use refined shea butter so that its normally strong, raw smell doesn't compete with the chocolate-scented cocoa butter and mint. If you prefer, though, unrefined shea will work just as well. Creamy cocoa and shea butters serve to protect and soothe skin while light and easily absorbed grapeseed oil helps offset the otherwise heavy richness of this recipe.

YIELD: FILLS 2 (4-OUNCE [120-ML]) JARS

1 oz (28 g) unrefined cocoa butter

1 oz (28 g) refined shea butter

2 oz (60 g) mint-infused grapeseed oil (see page 18 for how to infuse oil)

10 to 20 drops peppermint essential oil

1/8 to 1/4 tsp arrowroot powder (optional)

Place the cocoa and shea butters in a heatproof jar or container. Set the jar down in a saucepan containing a few inches (at least 5 cm) of water to form a makeshift double boiler. Place the pan over a medium-low burner until the butters have melted. Remove the pan from heat and add the mint-infused grapeseed oil.

Pour the melted butters and oil into a small mixing bowl and place in the refrigerator for about 45 minutes, or until it starts to firm up. Using a handheld or stand mixer, beat for several minutes or until light and fluffy, stopping to scrape the sides of the bowl several times.

Add the peppermint essential oil and arrowroot powder, then beat for another minute. A little bit of arrowroot powder or cornstarch added to body butters will help cut some of the oily feel they sometimes have, but it's an optional ingredient.

Store the finished butter in a glass jar in a cool, dark area away from high heat and direct sunlight. Shelf life should be around 6 months. If the butter gets too warm, it may melt. That's perfectly fine; just chill and whip it again. If you live in a cooler climate and find the butter is too hard, you may want to use more oil in the recipe.

Belly Butter for Expecting Moms

This whipped butter nourishes and moisturizes skin without any of the sketchy ingredients you might find in commercial products. It features cocoa butter and shea butter to keep your skin soft and supple. I use refined cocoa and shea butter for expecting moms, because those two ingredients have very little scent that might trigger nausea. Unrefined cocoa butter has a noticeable chocolate-like scent, while unrefined shea butter has a strong earthy scent that may be off-putting to sensitive noses. The sweet almond or sunflower oil is infused with calendula flowers to soothe itchy skin. Other good choices include violet leaves or chamomile. Grapeseed oil lightens the feel of the butter because it absorbs into your skin so quickly, but you could use jojoba oil or more infused oil in its place. Rosehip seed oil adds a special touch: it's rich in antioxidants and is a renowned skin healer, helping to improve damaged or scarred skin.

YIELD: FILLS 2 (4-OUNCE [120-ML]) JARS

0.85 oz (24 g) cocoa butter

3.7 oz (105 g) shea butter

1 oz (28 g) calendula-infused sweet almond or sunflower oil (see page 18 for how to infuse oil)

1 oz (28 g) grapeseed or jojoba oil or more infused oil

0.5 oz (14 g) rosehip seed oil

In a wide-mouth pint (500-ml) heatproof jar, combine the cocoa butter, shea butter, infused oil and grapeseed oil. Rosehip seed oil is heat sensitive, so it will be used later in the recipe. The jar is perfectly sized to melt and mix the contents in the same container by using one beater attached to a hand mixer. Place the jar in a saucepan containing a few inches (at least 5 cm) of water, forming a makeshift double boiler. Heat over medium-low heat until the butters are melted.

Remove the container from the heat and let cool for about 3 minutes. Stir in the rosehip seed oil. Chill the mixture in the refrigerator for 30 to 35 minutes, or until it starts solidifying.

Using one beater in a hand mixer, whip on medium-high to high speed until the texture is light and fluffy. If it seems too soft to hold a peak, put the container back in the refrigerator for another 5 to 10 minutes, then try whipping again.

Store the butter in the jar used for mixing, or spoon into jars and cover with their tops. Store in a cool, dry place out of direct sunlight. Shelf life is 6 months or more. Twice a day, rub over your stomach or any other areas you'd like to prevent stretch marks during pregnancy. You don't have to be pregnant to enjoy the protective skin-softening properties of this balm!

Calendula Whipped Coconut Oil

Calendula flowers are a wonderful addition to skin-care recipes because of their regenerating and healing properties. Coconut oil is antibacterial, anti-inflammatory and helps moisturize and protect skin. This simple recipe combines those two powerful ingredients, creating a great all-over body moisturizer that's perfect for use during winter and the cooler months of the year. In hot weather and climates, it will melt into a liquid, so you might want to consider making Calendula Whipped Coconut Butter on the following page instead.

YIELD: FILLS 2 (2-OUNCE [60-ML]) JARS

¼ cup (2 g) dried calendula flowers

½ cup (100 g) coconut oil

Place the dried flowers in a heatproof canning jar or container. Set the jar on a digital scale and weigh the coconut oil into it.

Gently set the jar down in a saucepan containing 1 to 2 inches (2.5 to 5 cm) of water, then place the pan over a burner set to low. Keep the pan on the heat for 1 to 2 hours, or until the oil has taken on a yellow hue from the calendula flowers. Remove from heat and strain into a small mixing bowl.

Set the bowl in the refrigerator for 20 to 30 minutes or until it starts firming up. Remove from the refrigerator and beat the chilled oil with a handheld mixer until it's light and fluffy. This may take up to 5 minutes. Scoop the coconut oil into a jar and store in a cool area that stays less than 76°F (24°C), the melting point of coconut oil.

Variation: Dandelion flowers are another good choice for this recipe and will result in a similarly effective moisturizer.

Calendula Whipped Coconut Butter

While coconut oil on its own is a fabulous moisturizer for some skin types, it tends to turn into a liquid mess in warm weather. This body butter combines the calendula-infused coconut oil from the previous recipe with skin-nourishing shea butter, to make a still light and airy, yet more shelf-stable, end product. I like to scent this with just a few drops of sweet orange essential oil, but other good options include peppermint, lavender, rose, lime and litsea cubeba.

YIELD: FILLS 4 (2-OUNCE [60-ML]) JARS

½ cup (100 g) calendula-infused coconut oil (see previous recipe)

¼ cup (55 g) shea butter

Few drops of your favorite essential oil (optional)

Add the calendula-infused coconut oil and the shea butter to a heatproof canning jar or container. Set the jar down in a saucepan containing a few inches (at least 5 cm) of water to form a makeshift double boiler. Place the pan over a medium-low burner and heat just until the shea butter is melted, then remove it promptly from the heat source to prevent it from overheating and becoming grainy.

Pour the hot mixture into a small mixing bowl. Cool in the refrigerator for around 30 minutes or until it starts firming up. Using a hand mixer, beat until it's light and fluffy. Add a few drops of essential oil for scent, if you'd like, then whip a few seconds longer.

Spoon into jars and store in a cool location, out of direct heat and sunlight. Shelf life of body butters is usually around 6 months.

Make Your Own Body Butter

The following formula will help you create customized body butters to best suit your skin type and climate. Shea butter has a rich texture that stays on your skin, making it ideal for those with extra-dry skin or conditions such as eczema. Mango butter has a lighter feel and is absorbed slightly quicker. The types of oils you choose will also play a part in how quickly the body butter absorbs into your skin and which benefits it imparts. A good tactic is to combine quick-absorbing oils with a slower-absorbing oil to make sure your body butter doesn't turn out too oily-feeling, yet still gives the benefit of the heavier oils. To further enrich your body butter, you may wish to first infuse the oil with skin-loving herbs such as violet leaves, plantain, calendula, dandelion flowers or another plant from pages 10 to 17.

YIELD: FILLS 3$\frac{1}{2}$ (4-OUNCE [120-ML]) JARS

$\frac{3}{4}$ cup (141 g) shea or mango butter

4 to 5 tbsp (48 to 60 g) liquid oils of choice (see opposite page), divided

1 to 2 optional add-ins (see opposite page)

40 to 80 drops (1 to 2 g) essential oils (optional)

In a wide-mouth pint (500-ml) heatproof jar, combine the shea butter and 4 tablespoons (48 g) of oils. The jar is perfectly sized to melt and mix the contents in the same container by using one beater attached to a hand mixer. Place the jar in a saucepan containing a few inches (at least 5 cm) of water, forming a makeshift double boiler. Heat over very low heat just until the butter is melted. If you're using an optional add-in that should be stirred into the melted mixture, add it now.

Chill the mixture in the refrigerator for 30 to 35 minutes, or until it starts solidifying. Using one beater in a hand mixer, beat for 1 minute, then add the essential oils and any other optional add-in, if using. Continue whipping the butter on medium-high to high speed until the texture is light and fluffy, scraping the sides of the jar occasionally. If it seems too soft to hold a peak, put the container back in the refrigerator for another 5 to 10 minutes, then try whipping again. If you want a softer butter or live in a cold climate where body butters harden too much at room temperature, add the remaining tablespoon (12 g) of oil and mix until completely incorporated.

Store the butter in the jar used for mixing, or spoon into smaller jars and cover with their tops. Store in a cool, dry place out of direct sunlight. Shelf life is 6 months or more.

LIQUID OILS THAT ABSORB QUICKLY

Apricot kernel—revitalizes aged or dry skin

Argan—antiaging, anti-inflammatory

Fractionated coconut—makes products lighter and less oily feeling

Grapeseed—light and nongreasy, soothes inflammation

Jojoba—good for all skin types

Rice bran—helpful for dry or mature skin

LIQUID OILS THAT ABSORB SLOWLY

Avocado—repairs damaged skin, good for eczema

Hemp—rich and moisturizing, good for problem skin

Olive—rich in squalene and natural antioxidants

Sunflower—helpful for broken or irritated skin

Sweet almond—protects damaged skin, helps relieve itching

Tamanu—relieves eczema, psoriasis and troubled skin

ESSENTIAL OIL OPTIONS

Bergamot (bergapten-free)—uplifting citrus scent

Cedarwood Himalayan—soft, woodsy scent

Geranium—lovely rose-like fragrance

Lavender—a gentle, calming classic

Sweet orange—fresh, cheerful scent

OPTIONAL ADD-INS

$\frac{1}{4}$ to $\frac{1}{2}$ tsp rose clay or purple Brazilian clay: Add with the essential oil for natural pink or purple color.

$\frac{1}{4}$ tsp lanolin: Stir into the melted mixture, right before removing it from the heat. Helpful for dry or chapped skin.

1 vitamin E capsule or $\frac{1}{4}$ tsp vitamin E oil: Helps extend shelf life and is extra nourishing for your skin.

$\frac{1}{2}$ to 1 tsp zinc oxide powder: Add to the melted mixture before chilling. Soothes and protects irritated skin.

SAMPLE RECIPE COMBINATION IDEAS

CALENDULA ORANGE

$\frac{3}{4}$ cup (165 g) shea butter

3 tbsp (36 g) calendula-infused rice bran oil

1 tbsp (12 g) fractionated coconut oil

60 drops sweet orange essential oil

$\frac{1}{4}$ tsp vitamin E oil

SIMPLE LAVENDER

$\frac{3}{4}$ cup (165 g) shea butter

$\frac{1}{4}$ cup (48 g) apricot kernel oil

40 drops lavender essential oil

ROSE GARDEN BODY BUTTER

$\frac{3}{4}$ cup (141 g) mango butter

2 tbsp (24 g) rose petal—infused sunflower oil

2 tbsp (24 g) rice bran oil

30 drops geranium essential oil

10 drops lavender essential oil

$\frac{1}{2}$ tsp rose clay

Sunflower Lotion Bars

Lotion bars are convenient little items, perfect for rubbing over cracked, dry hands or other areas in need of softening. Tucked in a tin, they become more portable than lotions or creams, but are similarly effective at relieving chapped or sun-parched skin conditions. This lotion bar recipe contains nourishing shea butter and is boosted with skin-smoothing sunflower petals. If sunflowers aren't available, try dandelion or calendula flowers for a similar effect.

YIELD: ABOUT 10 MINI LOTION BARS, DEPENDING ON THE SIZE OF YOUR MOLD

1 oz (28 g) shea butter

0.7 oz (20 g) beeswax

0.85 oz (24 g) sunflower-infused olive oil (see page 18, for how to infuse oil)

Place the shea butter, beeswax and infused oil in a heatproof canning jar or container. You can also use an empty, unlined tin can for easy cleanup. Set the jar or can down in a saucepan containing 1 to 2 inches (2.5 to 5 cm) of water. Place the pan over a medium-low burner until the beeswax is melted. Remove from heat, stir and pour into molds. You can use any type and size of candy or silicone mold that you'd like, as long as it's heatproof. Small 1-inch (2.5-cm) candy molds will yield around 10 lotion bars while larger ones will yield fewer.

Once they're completely cool, unmold the lotion bars and store in a cool area, out of direct heat and sunlight. You can choose to store them in individual tins or to stack in a wide-mouth jar, with wax paper separating each layer.

To use, rub over your hands, elbows, knees and other dry skin areas. The heat from your body will quickly melt the lotion bar and leave a thin protective layer on your skin. For extremely dry and cracked hands in desperate need of relief, try using one lotion bar each night as you watch your favorite TV show. You should see significant improvement within a few days of consistent use.

Tip: To make these by volume, you can use 2 tablespoons (30 ml) of shea butter, 2 tablespoons (30 ml) of beeswax and 2 tablespoons (30 ml) of oil.

Violet Leaf Lotion Bars

Soothing and moisturizing violet leaf combines with rich and creamy mango butter in these handy little lotion bars. French green clay adds subtle color and helps to absorb the extra oiliness that lotion bars can sometimes leave behind, but if your skin is extremely dry, you may want to skip the clay. Use at least once daily on rough, dry spots in need of moisture. Lotion bars are especially effective for quickly getting winter-neglected feet into sandal-ready condition. Try rubbing one all over your feet before bedtime, paying special attention to your heels, then cover with a pair of socks. Get a good night's sleep and wake up to softer soles!

YIELD: 8 TO 10 MINI LOTION BARS, DEPENDING ON THE SIZE OF YOUR MOLD

0.8 oz (23 g) mango butter

0.6 oz (17 g) beeswax

0.6 oz (17 g) violet leaf—infused coconut oil (see page 18 for how to infuse oil)

¹/₂ tsp French green clay (optional)

Place the mango butter, beeswax, infused oil and French green clay in a heatproof jar or container. Set the jar down in a saucepan containing 1 to 2 inches (2.5 to 5 cm) of water. Place the pan over a medium-low burner until the beeswax is melted. Remove from heat, stir and pour into molds. You can use any type and size of candy or silicone mold, as long as it's heatproof. Small 1-inch (2.5-cm) candy molds will yield 8 to 10 lotion bars while larger ones will yield fewer.

Once they're set up and completely cool, unmold the lotion bars and store in a cool, dark place. To use, rub over your hands, elbows, knees and other dry skin areas. The heat from your body will quickly melt the lotion bar and leave a thin protective layer on your skin.

Variation: If you're allergic or don't want to use coconut oil, try babassu, sweet almond, sunflower, olive, jojoba, rice bran, apricot kernel, argan or avocado oil instead.

Cocoa Rose Lotion Bars

Creamy cocoa butter and rose-infused sweet almond oil make up these luscious lotion bars. Rose petals were chosen for this recipe because they're soothing and help tame inflamed skin conditions. Sweet almond oil is exceptional for its softening and conditioning properties and works well for most skin types, but if you're allergic to tree nuts, try avocado oil or sunflower oil instead. Rose kaolin clay adds an optional hint of color and helps minimize the oily feel that lotion bars sometimes have.

YIELD: 8 TO 10 MINI LOTION BARS

0.85 oz (24 g) cocoa butter

0.5 oz (15 g) beeswax

0.8 oz (23 g) rose-infused sweet almond oil (see page 18 for how to infuse oil)

½ tsp rose kaolin clay (optional)

3 to 4 drops geranium or rose essential oil (optional)

Place the cocoa butter, beeswax, infused oil and rose kaolin clay in a heatproof jar or container. Set the jar down in a saucepan containing 1 to 2 inches (2.5 to 5 cm) of water. Place the pan over a medium-low burner until the cocoa butter and beeswax are melted. Remove from heat. If you'd like your lotion bars to be scented, stir in a few drops of essential oil at this time. Pour into molds. You can use any type and size of candy or silicone mold that you'd like as long as it's heatproof. Small 1-inch (2.5-cm) candy molds will yield 8 to 10 lotion bars while larger ones will yield fewer.

Once they've set up and are completely firm, unmold the lotion bars and store in a cool, dark place. To use, rub over your hands, elbows, knees and other dry skin areas. The heat from your body will slightly melt the outside layer of the lotion bar and leave it behind on your skin to moisturize and protect.

Tip: Cocoa butter comes in two forms, refined and unrefined. A high-quality unrefined cocoa butter will smell so deliciously of chocolate, you'll want to take a bite of it! A few people find this scent unpleasant, though, so if you're one of those, use refined, unscented cocoa butter or similar acting kokum butter instead.

Warm Toes Lotion Bar

If you tend to have cold feet, especially in the winter, then this lotion bar was created just for you! Coconut oil is first infused with two kitchen spices that promote warmth and circulation, plus calendula flowers for their skin-soothing properties. The infused oil is then mixed with shea butter and beeswax to form a solid bar that can be rubbed over cold feet. The heat from your skin will melt the surface of the bar just enough to leave a balm-like layer behind on your skin. Follow with a pair of socks to keep your feet toasty warm. This lotion bar might also be helpful on arthritic joints, but be sure to keep away from sensitive areas and don't rub in your eyes as it will sting. If you have neuropathy, diabetes or circulatory health conditions, check with your health care provider before use.

YIELD: 3 (1.5-OUNCE [43-G]) BARS

¼ cup (52 g) melted coconut oil

1 tsp ground ginger

1 tsp ground cayenne powder

5 to 6 dried calendula flowers (optional)

¼ cup (55 g) shea butter

¼ cup (29 g) packed beeswax pastilles

35 drops sweet orange essential oil (optional)

6 drops cinnamon leaf essential oil (optional)

Pour the coconut oil into a small half-pint (250-ml) canning jar. Add the ground ginger, cayenne and calendula, if using. Stir well. Infuse the oil using the quick method on page 19. Strain the finished oil through a fine mesh sieve into a new jar, leaving behind the layer of oily powder behind in the jar. You may have to strain a second or third time, to get most of the herb speckles strained out of the oil.

Add the shea butter and beeswax to the infused coconut oil and return it to the saucepan with water that was used to infuse the oil. Heat over a medium-low burner until the beeswax melts, 30 to 40 minutes.

Remove the melted mixture from the heat and cool for 10 minutes. Stir in the essential oils, if using, and pour into molds. Place the molds in the refrigerator for 30 to 45 minutes, or until the bars can easily be removed.

Store in tins or jars. Shelf life is at least 6 to 9 months, if stored in a cool location, out of direct sunlight.

Easy, All-Natural Creams & Lotions

Many people feel uncomfortable with the long list of synthetic chemicals printed on the bottle of lotion they slather on daily, but it seems too complicated a product to try to duplicate at home. I hope this chapter helps put that thought to rest!

With the use of a basic vegetable-derived emulsifying wax, you can quickly and easily put together a lotion that's custom-made for your skin type. Because emulsifying wax allows you to incorporate more water into a recipe than beeswax does, you should find these lotions to be light, moisturizing and easily absorbed.

Because I also know that some people prefer the use and feel of beeswax, I've included a few beeswax-only recipes as well, with the caveat that they're a little fussier to make, but worth the effort once mastered. Because beeswax isn't a true emulsifier and can't support the amount of water that emulsifying wax can, those recipes will feel richer, heavier and more cream-like.

Homemade creams and lotions are perishable and will spoil easily. I've given preservative recommendations for each recipe to extend shelf life. If you choose not to add a preservative, keep your lotion or cream in the refrigerator and use within one week. See page 26 for more information on preserving and extending the shelf life of your handmade creations.

Wildflowers in May Lotion

This lotion features a trio of flowers I discovered blooming near my house one beautiful day in May. The texture is light and will leave your skin feeling soft and moisturized. Elderflowers are a classic remedy our great-grandmothers used for clearer skin, while roses are the quintessential skin-care flower, soothing redness and heat. Honeysuckle is better known for treating colds when taken internally, but has also been shown to have anti-inflammatory and skin-conditioning properties when applied externally. For best results, use a scale to weigh the ingredients for this lotion. I've also included approximate volume measurements for those without a scale.

YIELD: 3½ OUNCES (100 ML)

½ cup (107 g) sunflower oil

1 tbsp (1 g) dried elderflowers

1 tbsp (1 g) dried rose petals

1 tbsp (1 g) dried honeysuckle flowers

1 tbsp plus ½ tsp (7 g) emulsifying wax

3 tbsp (44 g) distilled water

1 tbsp plus 2 tsp (25 g) rose hydrosol

Preservative of choice (see tip)

Using one of the methods on page 18, infuse the sunflower oil with the dried flowers. Strain out and reserve 1 tablespoon plus 2½ teaspoons (23 g) of the finished oil to use in this recipe. You can replace the amount of oil used from the infusing jar with fresh sunflower oil to continue the infusion for future projects.

Combine the 1 tablespoon plus 2½ teaspoons (23 g) of infused oil and the emulsifying wax in a half-pint (250-ml) canning jar. Measure out the water and hydrosol in a separate half-pint (250-ml) jar, and cover loosely with a canning lid to prevent evaporation as it heats. Set both jars down in a small saucepan containing 1 to 2 inches (2.5 to 5 cm) of water. Place the pan over a medium-low burner until the wax is melted, about 15 minutes.

Remove from heat and carefully pour the two mixtures together. Stir briskly and frequently with a fork as the lotion cools. Place the mixing container down in a bowl of ice water to speed up this step.

Once the lotion has cooled below 104°F (40°C), stir in the preservative. Pour the lotion into airless pump bottles, glass jars or your preferred containers. Depending on your brand of emulsifying wax, the lotion may take up to 24 hours to reach its final thickness.

Tip: For a nature-derived preservative option and a shelf life of around 2 months, use 4 grams (1 tsp) of Leucidal SF Max to prevent bacteria plus 2 g (½ tsp) of AMTicide Coconut to naturally prevent mold. For a longer shelf life of 6 to 9 months, use 1 g (¼ tsp) of Optiphen Plus, which is not considered all-natural, but is paraben-free and formaldehyde-free. If you choose to omit preservatives, store the lotion in the refrigerator and use within 1 week.

Basic Calendula Lotion

This simple lotion, featuring healing calendula flowers and skin-softening sweet almond oil, is gentle enough for everyone in the family to use. The basic recipe can also be used as a formula to help you branch out and create your own individualized variations. You can substitute calendula with your favorite herb or flower, use any type of liquid carrier oil that you like and substitute part of the water with witch hazel or aloe instead. Add a few drops of your favorite essential oil for scent and you will have your very own personalized lotion! For best results, use a digital scale to weigh the ingredients for this lotion. I've also included approximate volume measurements for those without a scale.

YIELD: 3½ OUNCES (100 ML)

1½ tbsp (19 g) calendula-infused sweet almond oil (see page 18 for how to infuse oil)

1 tbsp plus ½ tsp (7 g) emulsifying wax NF

5 tbsp (75 g) distilled water

Preservative of choice (see tip)

Combine the infused oil and emulsifying wax in a half-pint (250-ml) canning jar. Measure out the water in a separate half-pint (250-ml) jar, and cover loosely with a canning lid to prevent evaporation as it heats. Set both jars down in a small saucepan containing 1 to 2 inches (2.5 to 5 cm) of water. Place the pan over a medium-low burner until the wax is melted, about 15 minutes.

Remove from heat and carefully pour the two mixtures together. Stir briskly and frequently with a fork as the lotion cools. Place the mixing container down in a bowl of ice water to speed up this step.

Once the lotion has cooled below 104°F (40°C), stir in the preservative. Pour the lotion into airless pump bottles, glass jars or your preferred containers. Depending on your brand of emulsifying wax, the lotion may take up to 24 hours to reach its final thickness.

Tip: For a nature-derived preservative option and shelf life of around 2 months, use 4 grams (1 tsp) of Leucidal SF Max to prevent bacteria plus 2 g (½ tsp) of AMTicide Coconut, to naturally prevent mold. For a longer shelf life of 6 to 9 months, use 1 g (¼ tsp) of Optiphen Plus, which is not considered all-natural, but is paraben-free and formaldehyde-free. If you choose to omit preservatives, store the lotion in the refrigerator and use within 1 week.

Sleepy Time Lotion

This calming lotion features skin-soothing herbs and is scented with the same trio of essential oils used in Sleepy Time Bath Bombs (page 134). Sweet orange helps release stress and anxiety, while lavender helps your mind relax and calms the nervous system. Vetiver is deeply relaxing and is sometimes used to treat insomnia; if it's not available, it can easily be left out of the recipe. If using on children ages two to six, reduce the essential oil amount by half. A small amount of fractionated coconut oil is included in the recipe to make the lotion absorb more quickly into your skin, but another quick-absorbing oil, such as jojoba or grapeseed, or more infused oil, can be substituted in its place. For best results, use a scale to weigh the ingredients for this lotion. I've also included approximate volume measurements for those without a scale.

YIELD: $3^{1}/_{2}$ OUNCES (100 ML)

1 tbsp plus $1^{1}/_{4}$ tsp (18 g) plantain-, violet leaf- or lavender-infused sunflower oil (see page 18 for how to infuse oil)

$1^{1}/_{4}$ tsp (5 g) fractionated coconut oil or more infused oil

1 tbsp plus $^{1}/_{2}$ tsp (7 g) emulsifying wax

$^{1}/_{4}$ cup plus $^{3}/_{4}$ tsp (64 g) distilled water

22 drops lavender essential oil

6 drops sweet orange essential oil

1 drop vetiver essential oil (optional)

Preservative of choice (see tip)

Combine the infused oil, fractionated coconut oil and emulsifying wax in a half-pint (250-ml) canning jar. Measure out the water in a separate half-pint (250-ml) jar, and cover loosely with a canning lid to prevent evaporation as it heats. Set both jars down in a small saucepan containing 1 to 2 inches (2.5 to 5 cm) of water. Place the pan over a medium-low burner and heat until the wax is melted, about 15 minutes.

Remove from heat and carefully pour the two mixtures together. Stir briskly and frequently with a fork as the lotion cools. Place the mixing container down in a bowl of ice water to speed up this step.

Once the lotion has cooled below 104°F (40°C), stir in the essential oils and preservative. Pour the lotion into airless pump bottles, glass jars or your preferred containers. Depending on your brand of emulsifying wax, the lotion may take up to 24 hours to reach its final thickness.

Tip: For a nature-derived preservative option and shelf life of around 2 months, use 4 grams (1 tsp) of Leucidal SF Max to prevent bacteria plus 2 g ($^{1}/_{2}$ tsp) of AMTicide Coconut, to naturally prevent mold. For a longer shelf life of 6 to 9 months, use 1 g ($^{1}/_{4}$ tsp) of Optiphen Plus, which is not considered all-natural, but is paraben-free and formaldehyde-free. If you choose to omit preservatives, store the lotion in the refrigerator and use within 1 week.

Aloe Mint After-Sun Lotion

The menthol in mint makes this lotion especially cooling, while aloe helps soothe overheated, inflamed skin tissue. Sunflower oil was chosen for this recipe as it's particularly effective at healing damaged skin. A few drops of peppermint essential oil contribute a heightened chilling effect along with a dash of mild pain relief. Apply this lotion as often as needed to help ease the discomfort of sunburn and other hot, flushed skin conditions. Don't feel that it's limited to sunburn relief though; it's perfect for helping you keep your cool every day during the summer months as well! For best results, use a digital scale to weigh the ingredients for this lotion. I've also included approximate volume measurements for those without a scale.

YIELD: 4 OUNCES (120 ML)

4 tsp (17 g) mint-infused sunflower oil (see page 18 for how to infuse oil)

3 tsp (6 g) emulsifying wax NF

1/4 cup (60 g) distilled water

2 tbsp (26 g) aloe vera gel

2 to 3 drops peppermint essential oil

Preservative of choice (see tip)

Combine the infused oil and emulsifying wax in a half-pint (250-ml) canning jar. Measure out the water and aloe vera gel in a separate half-pint (250-ml) jar, and cover loosely with a canning lid to prevent evaporation as it heats. Set both jars down in a small saucepan containing 1 to 2 inches (2.5 to 5 cm) of water. Place the pan over a medium-low burner until the wax is melted, about 15 minutes.

Remove from heat and carefully pour the two mixtures together. Stir briskly and frequently with a fork as the lotion cools. Place the mixing container down in a bowl of ice water to speed up this step.

Once the lotion has cooled below 104°F (40°C), stir in the essential oil and preservative. Pour the lotion into airless pump bottles, glass jars or your preferred containers. Depending on your brand of emulsifying wax, the lotion may take up to 24 hours to reach its final thickness.

Tip: For a nature-derived preservative option and shelf life of around 2 months, use 4 grams (1 tsp) of Leucidal SF Max to prevent bacteria plus 2 g (1/2 tsp) of AMTicide Coconut, to naturally prevent mold. For a longer shelf life of 6 to 9 months, use 1 g (1/4 tsp) of Optiphen Plus, which is not considered all-natural, but is paraben-free and formaldehyde-free. If you choose to omit preservatives, store the lotion in the refrigerator and use within 1 week.

Grapeseed & Thyme Lotion

This lightweight lotion is specially designed for those with oily and acne-prone skin. Grapeseed is a hypoallergenic, nongreasy oil that absorbs into your skin quickly. In this recipe, it's paired with thyme, an herb known for its ability to effectively wipe out the bacteria that cause acne. Witch hazel is an astringent that tones skin while reducing redness and inflammation. For an extra antibacterial boost, try adding a drop or two of tea tree oil. Lightly smooth this lotion over your face and neck daily, or as needed, for softer skin. For best results, use a digital scale to weigh the ingredients for this lotion. I've also included approximate volume measurements for those without a scale.

YIELD: 3½ OUNCES (100 ML)

1 tbsp (13 g) thyme-infused grapeseed oil (see page 18 for how to infuse oil)

3 tsp (6 g) emulsifying wax NF

¼ cup (60 g) distilled water

1½ tbsp (17 g) witch hazel

1 to 2 drops tea tree essential oil (optional)

Preservative of choice (see tip)

Combine the infused oil and emulsifying wax in a half-pint (250-ml) canning jar. Measure out the water and witch hazel in a separate half-pint (250-ml) jar, and cover loosely with a canning lid to prevent evaporation as it heats. Set both jars down in a small saucepan containing 1 to 2 inches (2.5 to 5 cm) of water. Place the pan over a medium-low burner until the wax is melted, about 15 minutes.

Remove from heat and carefully pour the two mixtures together. Stir briskly and frequently with a fork as the lotion cools. Place the mixing container down in a bowl of ice water to speed up this step.

Once the lotion has cooled below 104°F (40°C), stir in the essential oil, if using, and preservative. Pour the lotion into airless pump bottles, glass jars or your preferred containers. Depending on your brand of emulsifying wax, the lotion may take up to 24 hours to reach its final thickness.

Tip: For a nature-derived preservative option and shelf life of around 2 months, use 4 grams (1 tsp) of Leucidal SF Max to prevent bacteria plus 2 g (½ tsp) of AMTicide Coconut, to naturally prevent mold. For a longer shelf life of 6 to 9 months, use 1 g (¼ tsp) of Optiphen Plus, which is not considered all-natural, but is paraben-free and formaldehyde-free. If you choose to omit preservatives, store the lotion in the refrigerator and use within
1 week.

Oatmeal & Chickweed Eczema Cream

This soothing cream features colloidal oatmeal, an ultra-fine, silky powder that is commercially milled from oats. Colloidal oatmeal can be purchased from specialty online shops (see page 330), or check the bath products section of local stores for soothing bath treatment packets that contain only 100 percent colloidal oatmeal. Colloidal oatmeal has been shown to be effective for treating mild to moderate eczema when used at 1 percent of a lotion or cream recipe. I coupled it with two spring herbs, chickweed and violet leaves, which calm and soothe irritated skin conditions. For best results, use a scale to weigh the ingredients for this cream.

YIELD: 3½ OUNCES (100 ML)

½ cup (107 g) sunflower oil

2 tbsp (2 g) dried chickweed

2 tbsp (2 g) dried violet leaves

½ tbsp (7 g) shea butter

1 tbsp plus ½ tsp (7 g) emulsifying wax

¼ cup plus 1 tsp (66 g) distilled water

½ tsp colloidal oatmeal

2 to 3 drops lavender essential oil (optional)

Preservative of choice (see tip)

Using one of the methods on page 18, infuse the sunflower oil with the dried herbs. Strain out and reserve 1 tablespoon plus 1 teaspoon (17 g) of the finished oil to use in this recipe.

Combine the 1 tablespoon plus 1 teaspoon (17 g) of infused oil with the shea butter and emulsifying wax in a half-pint (250-ml) canning jar. Measure out the water in a separate half-pint (250-ml) jar and stir in the colloidal oatmeal. Cover the water and oatmeal jar loosely with a canning lid to prevent evaporation as it heats.

Set both jars down in a small saucepan containing 1 to 2 inches (2.5 to 5 cm) of water, then place the pan over a medium-low burner and heat until the wax has melted, about 15 minutes.

Remove from heat and carefully pour the two mixtures together. Stir briskly and frequently with a fork as the cream cools. Place the mixing container down in a bowl of ice water to speed up this step.

Once the cream has cooled below 104°F (40°C), stir in the essential oil, if using, and preservative. Pour the cream into airless pump bottles, glass jars or your preferred containers. Depending on your brand of emulsifying wax, the cream may take up to 24 hours to reach its final thickness.

Tip: For a nature-derived preservative option and shelf life of around 2 months, use 4 grams (1 tsp) of Leucidal SF Max to prevent bacteria plus 2 g (½ tsp) of AMTicide Coconut, to naturally prevent mold. For a longer shelf life of 6 to 9 months, use 1 g (¼ tsp) of Optiphen Plus, which is not considered all-natural, but is paraben-free and formaldehyde-free. If you choose to omit preservatives, store the cream in the refrigerator and use within 1 week.

Sunflower & Sweet Orange Cream

This cream makes me think of sunshine and happiness! Skin-conditioning sunflower petals are infused within, but you could also use calendula, chamomile, forsythia or dandelion flowers in their place. Sweet orange essential oil adds a bright cheerful scent and a few optional drops of litsea (may chang) essential oil help round out the overall fragrance. This makes a great daily moisturizer to uplift the mood and inspire productive energy. For best results, use a scale to weigh the ingredients for this cream. I've also included approximate volume measurements for those without a scale.

YIELD: 3½ OUNCES (100 ML)

1½ tbsp (19 g) sunflower-infused sunflower oil (see page 18 for how to infuse oil)

½ tbsp (7 g) mango or shea butter

1 tbsp plus 1 tsp (9 g) emulsifying wax

¼ cup plus 1 tbsp (75 g) distilled water

22 drops sweet orange essential oil

2 drops litsea essential oil (optional)

Preservative of choice (see tip)

Combine the infused oil, butter and wax in a half-pint (250-ml) canning jar. Measure out the water in a separate half-pint (250-ml) jar, and cover loosely with a canning lid to prevent evaporation as it heats. Set both jars down in a saucepan containing 1 to 2 inches (2.5 to 5 cm) of water. Place the pan over a medium-low burner until the wax is melted, about 15 minutes.

Remove from heat and carefully pour the two mixtures together. Stir briskly and frequently with a fork as the cream cools. Place the mixing container down in a bowl of ice water to speed up this step.

Once the cream has cooled below 104°F (40°C), stir in the essential oils and preservative. Pour the cream into airless pump bottles, glass jars or your preferred containers. Depending on your brand of emulsifying wax, the cream may take up to 24 hours to reach its final thickness.

Tip: For a nature-derived preservative option and shelf life of around 2 months, use 4 grams (1 tsp) of Leucidal SF Max to prevent bacteria plus 2 g (½ tsp) of AMTicide Coconut, to naturally prevent mold. For a longer shelf life of 6 to 9 months, use 1 g (¼ tsp) of Optiphen Plus, which is not considered all-natural, but is paraben-free and formaldehyde-free. If you choose to omit preservatives, store the cream in the refrigerator and use within 1 week.

➵ See photo on page 106.

Rose Face Cream

This naturally colored face cream is a treat for mature skin! Roses are cooling and soothing, making them a wonderful ingredient in skin-care products. Sweet almond oil is suitable for most skin types, high in beneficial fatty acids and helps soften and improve skin texture. Shea butter is high in vitamins A and E and is especially useful for treating weathered and damaged skin. Witch hazel tones and fights inflammation. For best results, use a digital scale to weigh the ingredients for this cream.

YIELD: 4 OUNCES (120 ML)

¼ cup (4 g) loosely packed fresh or dried rose petals

¼ cup (60 g) simmering hot distilled water

1 tbsp (13 g) sweet almond oil

1 tbsp (14 g) shea butter

1 tbsp plus ½ tsp (7 g) emulsifying wax NF

Tiny pinch of alkanet root, for color (optional)

2 tbsp (23 g) witch hazel

2 to 3 drops rose or geranium rose essential oil (optional)

Preservative of choice (see tip)

FOR THE ROSE-INFUSED WATER

Place the rose petals in a half-pint (250-ml) canning jar and pour the simmering hot water over them. Let steep for 20 minutes. Strain.

FOR THE CREAM

Combine the oil, shea butter and emulsifying wax in a heatproof half-pint (250-ml) jar. If you'd like your cream tinted pale pink, add a small pinch of alkanet root to the oil. Add the witch hazel to the separate jar of rose-infused water, and cover it loosely with a canning lid to prevent water evaporation as it heats. Set both jars down in a small saucepan containing 1 to 2 inches (2.5 to 5 cm) of water. Place the pan over a medium-low burner until the wax is melted, about 15 minutes.

Remove from heat and carefully pour the two mixtures together. Stir briskly and frequently with a fork as the cream cools. Place the mixing container down in a bowl of ice water to speed up this step. Once the cream has cooled below 104°F (40°C), stir in the essential oil, if using, and preservative. Pour the cream into glass jars or your preferred containers. Depending on your brand of emulsifying wax, the cream may take up to 24 hours to reach its final thickness.

Tip: For a nature-derived preservative option and shelf life of around 2 months, use 4 grams (1 tsp) of Leucidal SF Max to prevent bacteria plus 2 g (½ tsp) of AMTicide Coconut, to naturally prevent mold. For a longer shelf life of 6 to 9 months, use 1 g (¼ tsp) of Optiphen Plus, which is not considered all-natural, but is paraben-free and formaldehyde-free. If you choose to omit preservatives, store the cream in the refrigerator and use within 1 week.

Honey & Chamomile Cream

This thick, rich face and body cream is ideal for those with damaged or weathered skin. It also can be used as an aid to relieve the discomfort of eczema and other itchy, dry skin afflictions. It contains chamomile, a wonderful herb with mild cortisone-like properties, along with sunflower oil, which has been shown to be an effective skin healer. Raw honey fights skin inflammation and repairs skin, while nourishing shea butter softens and protects from further damage. Lavender essential oil not only contributes a calming scent, but soothes and relieves hot, inflamed skin conditions. Because this cream is so rich, it does best when applied at bedtime, so it has time to sink into your skin overnight.

YIELD: 5 OUNCES (150 ML)

2 oz (57 g) chamomile-infused sunflower oil (see page 18 for how to infuse oil)

1 oz (28 g) shea butter

0.5 oz (14 g) beeswax, grated or pastilles

1.75 oz (50 g) warm distilled water

1 tsp raw honey

2 to 3 drops lavender essential oil (optional)

Preservative of choice (see tip)

Place the chamomile-infused oil, butter and beeswax in a heatproof jar or container. Set the jar down in a saucepan containing a few inches (7 cm) of water. Place the pan over a medium-low burner until the wax and butter are melted. Remove from heat, pour into a small mixing bowl and let cool to 85 to 95°F (29 to 35°C).

While the oil mixture is cooling, stir the warm water and honey together in a small bowl or cup until the honey is fully dissolved. Set aside.

Once the oil mixture has sufficiently cooled, it will be thicker and almost salve-like. Check the temperature of the water and heat if necessary by setting it down in the pan of water used to melt the beeswax and oils. When making creams with beeswax and no emulsifier, it's important that both the oil and water portions are in the same temperature range of 85 to 95°F (29 to 35°C) and less than 5 degrees apart for the most successful emulsion.

Using a hand mixer, start beating the oil mixture. Continue beating, adding a small amount of water at a time and incorporating it before adding more. It may take up to a minute to incorporate. Add the essential oil, if using, and the preservative. Continue beating another 3 to 5 minutes, stopping to scrape down the sides of the bowl once or twice. Spoon the cream into glass jars or your preferred containers.

Tip: For a nature-derived preservative option and shelf life of around 2 months, use 6 grams (1½ tsp) of Leucidal SF Max to prevent bacteria plus 3 g (¾ tsp) of AMTicide Coconut, to naturally prevent mold. For a longer shelf life of 6 to 9 months, use 1.5 g (¼ plus tsp) of Optiphen Plus, which is not considered all-natural, but is paraben-free and formaldehyde-free. If you choose to omit preservatives, store the cream in the refrigerator and use within 1 week.

Elderflower Eye Cream

This eye cream contains luxurious oils designed to help fight the signs of aging. Argan is a premier oil that improves and repairs skin texture. If it's difficult to obtain, you can use easily absorbed sweet almond or rice bran oil instead, although they won't have the potent benefits that argan oil does. Elderflowers are an old-fashioned remedy for a beautiful, clear complexion, while modern research has shown them to possess antioxidants and anti-inflammatory properties as well. Rosehip seed oil is one of the best, most effective antiaging oils around. It helps regenerate skin tissue, reduce the appearance of scars and smooth out wrinkles. Mango butter is yet another wrinkle fighter that softens and conditions skin as well.

YIELD: 2 OUNCES (60 ML)

0.5 oz (14 g) elderflower-infused argan oil (see page 18 for how to infuse oil)

0.5 oz (14 g) mango butter

0.5 oz (14 g) beeswax, grated or pastilles

0.5 oz (14 g) rosehip seed oil

1½ tbsp (22 ml) distilled water

Preservative of choice (see tip)

Place the elderflower-infused argan oil, butter and beeswax in a heatproof jar or container. Because rosehip seed oil is heat sensitive, save it for later in the recipe. Set the jar down in a saucepan that has 1 to 2 inches (2.5 to 5 cm) of water in the bottom. Place the pan over a medium-low burner and heat until the wax has melted. Remove from heat and stir in the rosehip seed oil. Let cool to 85 to 95°F (29 to 35°C).

In a small saucepan, heat the water slightly until it matches the temperature of the oil. The oil and water portions really need to be within 5 degrees Fahrenheit (about 3 degrees Celsius) of each other for the most successful emulsion.

Slowly drizzle the water into the oil mixture as you beat it with a handheld mixer. It may take 30 to 45 seconds to accomplish this step. Beat for 5 to 10 minutes or until a thick cream develops.

Add the preservative and beat well for 15 to 30 seconds to completely incorporate. Spoon the cream into glass jars or your preferred containers.

Tip: For a nature-derived preservative option and shelf life of around 2 months, use 3 grams (¾ tsp) of Leucidal SF Max to prevent bacteria plus 2 g (½ tsp) of AMTicide Coconut, to naturally prevent mold. For a longer shelf life of 6 to 9 months, use 1 g (¼ tsp) of Optiphen Plus, which is not considered all-natural, but is paraben-free and formaldehyde-free. If you choose to omit preservatives, store the cream in the refrigerator and use within 1 week.

Variation: If elderflowers aren't available, roses, chamomile, calendula and violets share similar complexion-improving properties.

Quick, Custom Herbal Cream

This simplified cream recipe designed for beginners comes together quickly, with no special emulsifiers, wax or equipment needed. It yields a thick, creamy moisturizer with a pleasing silky feel when rubbed between your fingers and over your skin. While you can add other water-based ingredients, such as rose water or witch hazel, a thick aloe vera gel tends to bring something special to this cream and yields the best results. Some herbs and flowers that do well in this recipe include, but aren't limited to, lavender, rose, forsythia, dandelion, calendula, chamomile, mint and violet leaves.

YIELD: ALMOST FILLS A 2-OUNCE (60-ML) JAR

2 tbsp (30 ml) flower or herb-infused oil of your choice (see page 18 for how to infuse oil)

1 tbsp (14 g) shea or mango butter

1 tbsp (15 ml) aloe vera gel

2 to 3 drops essential oil (optional)

Preservative of choice (see tip)

Review the flowers and herbs on pages 10 to 17 and oils on pages 19 to 21 and choose the ones you'd like for your cream, then infuse the oil with the plants. Add the flower or herb-infused oil and butter to a half-pint (250-ml) canning jar. Set the jar down in a small saucepan containing 1 to 2 inches (2.5 to 5 cm) of water and heat until the butter is melted. Remove from heat and place the mixture in the refrigerator for 30 to 45 minutes, or until it firms up to the consistency of a soft salve.

Using a fork, stir well. Add the aloe, essential oil and preservative, then stir vigorously for about 2 minutes. The mixture will start to turn opaque and creamy. Set it aside for 5 to 10 minutes to thicken, then stir thoroughly once more with the fork. You should now have a thickened cream.

Store the cream in a cool area or your refrigerator. If the quick cream begins to separate, simply whisk with a fork again until blended back together.

Smooth this cream over your hands, face and body, preferably after a bath or shower to seal in the moisture. Because of the small amount of liquid in this cream, it's very rich—a little bit goes a long way!

Tip: For a nature-derived preservative option and shelf life of around 2 months, use 2 grams ($^1/_2$ tsp) of Leucidal SF Max to prevent bacteria plus 1 g ($^1/_4$ tsp) of AMTicide Coconut, to naturally prevent mold. For a longer shelf life of 6 to 9 months, use 0.5 g ($^1/_8$ tsp) of Optiphen Plus, which is not considered all-natural, but is paraben-free and formaldehyde-free. If you choose to omit preservatives, store the cream in the refrigerator and use within 1 week.

Violet & Aloe Moisturizing Cream

This recipe incorporates the Violet-Infused Aloe from page 51. While infused aloe alone is a soothing treat for inflamed skin, it works equally well for daily skin protection when incorporated in moisturizing creams such as this one. Stearic acid (a natural fatty acid sourced from plants or animals) is a popular ingredient used to help thicken creams and lotions. If you leave it out, the recipe will yield unreliable results. Sweet almond oil is high in nourishing fatty acids and helps soften and smooth skin, while shea butter protects against damaging elements. For best results, use a digital scale to weigh the ingredients for this cream. I've also included approximate volume measurements for those without a scale.

YIELD: 3 OUNCES (90 ML)

3 tbsp (39 g) sweet almond oil

1½ tbsp (21 g) shea butter

1 tbsp (10 g) tightly packed beeswax, grated or pastilles

½ tbsp (3 g) stearic acid

¼ cup (52 g) violet-infused aloe (or plain aloe vera gel)

Few drops of essential oil, for scent (optional)

Preservative of choice (see tip)

Combine the sweet almond oil, butter, beeswax and stearic acid in a heatproof jar or container. Set the jar down in a saucepan that has 1 to 2 inches (2.5 to 5 cm) of water in it. Place the pan over a medium-low burner until the wax and stearic acid are melted.

Remove from heat and pour into a small mixing bowl. Let cool to room temperature, then add the infused aloe vera gel and essential oil, if using. One of my favorite scent combinations for this cream is a few drops each of lavender and litsea cubeba essential oils, but you can use any scent that you prefer. Using a handheld mixer, beat for around 4 minutes. Add the preservative, then beat for an additional minute, or until thick and creamy. Spoon the finished cream into a glass jar.

Tip: For a nature-derived preservative option and shelf life of around 2 months, use 4 grams (1 tsp) of Leucidal SF Max to prevent bacteria plus 2 g (½ tsp) of AMTicide Coconut, to naturally prevent mold. For a longer shelf life of 6 to 9 months, use 1 g (¼ tsp) of Optiphen Plus, which is not considered all-natural, but is paraben-free and formaldehyde-free. If you choose to omit preservatives, store the cream in the refrigerator and use within 1 week.

Variation: Sweet almond oil is a great all-purpose oil suitable for most skin types, but if you're allergic to tree nuts, try using sunflower or avocado oil instead. Mango butter can be used if shea is not available or tolerated.

Garden-Fresh Bath Bombs, Soaks & Salts

Soak away the stresses of life with these herbal bath recipes designed to renew, revitalize or relax your mind, body and spirit.

For those times that you're in need of a quick pick-me-up, try Energizing Rosemary Mint Bath Tea (page 149) or Rise & Shine Shower Bombs (page 137).

Are you longing for a good night's sleep? You'll surely want to spend time relaxing in a Calming Bath Soak (page 144) or drop a Sleepy Time Bath Bomb (page 134) in your tub. For an even greater sleep-inducing effect, try pairing one of these soothing bath treats with a spoonful of Chamomile Calming Syrup (page 285) or Sleepy Time Lotion (page 112).

If you're a bath bomb fan like me, I've got you covered! I've provided a super simple formula (page 138) to help you create your own bath bombs using basic ingredients from local stores, plus a handful of my tried-and-true recipes to jump-start your inspiration process.

Calendula Oatmeal Bath Bombs

These lovely bath bombs are filled with skin-soothing oatmeal and reparative calendula flowers, making them extra nice for itchy or dry skin types. Rich, creamy cocoa butter holds the bath bomb together in storage, then melts upon contact with warm bathwater, leaving behind a moisturizing and protective layer on your skin once you're done bathing. Leave these unscented or try adding an essential oil such as calming lavender or uplifting sweet orange.

YIELD: 5 BATH BOMBS

2 tbsp (14 g) rolled oats

1 tbsp (0.5 g) dried calendula petals

2 cups (572 g) baking soda

1 cup (236 g) citric acid

3 tbsp (30 g) cocoa butter, melted

20 drops sweet orange or lavender essential oil (optional)

Witch hazel in a small spray bottle (optional)

Coarsely ground oats and calendula petals for topping (optional)

½-cup (120-ml) measuring cup

Dinner plate

Wax paper, cut into 6-inch (15-cm) squares

Grind the rolled oats and calendula petals together in a coffee grinder until finely powdered. In a medium-sized mixing bowl, stir the baking soda, citric acid, powdered oats and calendula petals together, working out any clumps with your fingers. In a separate bowl, combine the melted cocoa butter with the essential oil, if using.

Slowly drizzle the melted cocoa butter into the combined dry ingredients while stirring with a whisk. Break up any remaining clumps with your hands to ensure the butter is completely incorporated.

Try squeezing a portion of the mixture into a ball shape. If it holds together without easily falling apart, it's ready to mold. If it crumbles, spray 2 to 3 spritzes of witch hazel into the mixture while stirring, then check again. Once the mixture holds together easily without crumbling, it's ready. Be sparing with the witch hazel, as too much will cause your bath bomb to prematurely expand or fall apart.

If you'd like to decorate the top of your bath bomb with ground oats and calendula petals, as shown in the photo, sprinkle a small amount in the bottom of the measuring cup. Keep the amount of topping light, as it will need to be cleaned from the tub after the bath. Next, fill the measuring cup with the mixture, pressing firmly as you pack it in.

Turn the dinner plate upside down on your work surface. Lay a square of wax paper on top, then turn out the bath bomb from the measuring cup and onto the wax paper. Gently slide the wax paper off the plate to the spot where you plan to let the bath bombs dry. Using the plate and wax paper in this way makes it much easier to move the bath bombs around.

Allow the bath bombs to air-dry for several hours, then wrap in airtight packaging. Be careful exiting the tub after use, as the tub floor may become slippery from the cocoa butter.

Sleepy Time Bath Bombs

Help promote a restful night's sleep by bathing with one of these relaxing bath bombs before bedtime. The recipe features simple sunflower oil that can be infused with a calming herb, such as chamomile or lemon balm, or you could try other sleep-promoting herbs such as lavender or valerian root. They're scented with an essential oil blend I've found helpful for my daughter, who has a very active mind and sometimes finds easy sleep to be elusive. Sweet orange helps to release stress and to reduce anxiety; vetiver is deeply relaxing and sometimes used to treat insomnia; lavender helps your mind relax and calms the nervous system. If vetiver is hard to source, it can easily be omitted from the recipe. I suggest not decorating the tops of these, so you don't have to worry about cleaning bits of flowers out of the tub when you'd rather be sleeping.

YIELD: 4 BATH BOMBS

1¾ cups (500 g) baking soda

1 cup (236 g) citric acid

½ cup (144 g) fine sea salt

2 tbsp (20 g) sunflower or other oil optionally infused with chamomile or lemon balm (see page 18 for how to infuse oil)

18 drops lavender essential oil

6 drops orange essential oil

1 drop vetiver essential oil (optional)

Witch hazel in a small spray bottle (optional)

½-cup (120-ml) measuring cup

Dinner plate

Wax paper, cut into 6-inch (15-cm) squares

In a medium-sized mixing bowl, stir the baking soda, citric acid and salt together, working out any clumps with your fingers. In a separate bowl, combine the oil with the essential oils.

Slowly drizzle the oil into the combined dry ingredients while stirring with a whisk. Break up any remaining clumps with your hands to ensure the oil is completely incorporated.

Try squeezing a portion of the mixture into a ball shape. If it holds together without easily falling apart, it's ready to mold. If it crumbles, spray 2 to 3 spritzes of witch hazel into the mixture while stirring, then check again. Once the mixture holds together easily without crumbling, it's ready. Be sparing with the witch hazel, as too much will cause your bath bomb to prematurely expand or fall apart.

Fill the measuring cup with the bath bomb mixture, pressing firmly as you pack it in. Turn the dinner plate upside down on your work surface. Lay a square of wax paper on top, then turn out the bath bomb from the measuring cup and onto the wax paper. Gently slide the wax paper off the plate to the spot where you plan to let the bath bombs dry. Using the plate and wax paper in this way makes it much easier to move the bath bombs around.

Allow the bath bombs to air-dry for several hours, then wrap in airtight packaging. Be careful exiting the tub after use, as the tub floor may become slippery from the oil.

Rise & Shine Shower Bombs

These fun shower bombs are scented with a cheerful blend of citrus essential oils. Grapefruit is refreshing and useful for lifting feelings of lethargy, while sweet orange promotes happiness and energy. They're the perfect way to start your day off right! Shower bombs are sometimes called shower steamers. They're made in a similar way to bath bombs, only they don't have added oil or butter because those would make the shower floor slippery. They also have a higher rate of essential oils than is skin-safe, so should only be used in showers for aromatherapy purposes, and not for bathing. Place a shower bomb in the far corner of your shower where indirect splashes from the water spray will slowly dissolve it, releasing the bright therapeutic aroma while you wash up. For best results, make on a dry day with low humidity or in a room with a dehumidifier.

YIELD: 5 SHOWER BOMBS

1 cup (286 g) baking soda

½ cup (118 g) citric acid

1 tbsp (6 g) white kaolin clay

¼ tsp yellow Brazilian clay (optional for color)

¾ tsp grapefruit essential oil

¾ tsp sweet orange essential oil

Dishwashing gloves or latex or nitrile gloves

Witch hazel in a small spray bottle

¼-cup (60-ml) measuring cup

Dinner plate

Wax paper, cut into 6-inch (15-cm) squares

In a medium-sized mixing bowl, stir the baking soda, citric acid and clays together with a whisk, working out any clumps with your fingers. Sprinkle in the essential oils, and work them in while wearing gloves to avoid skin contact with undiluted essential oils.

Spray 1 to 2 light spritzes of witch hazel into the mixture while stirring with a whisk. Try squeezing a portion of the mixture into a ball shape. If it holds together without easily falling apart, it's ready to mold. If it crumbles, spray another spritz of witch hazel into the mixture while stirring and check again. The mixture is ready when it holds together easily without crumbling. Don't add too much witch hazel or your shower bombs will expand prematurely.

Fill the measuring cup with the shower bomb mixture, pressing firmly as you pack it in. Turn the dinner plate upside down on your work surface. Lay a square of wax paper on top, then turn out the shower bomb from the measuring cup and onto the wax paper. Gently slide the wax paper off the plate to the spot where you plan to let the steamers dry. Using the plate and wax paper in this way makes it much easier to move the shower bombs around.

Allow them to air-dry for several hours, then wrap in airtight packaging.

Make Your Own Bath Bombs

Use this formula to design your own beautiful bath bomb creations. You'll be able to customize with your favorite herbs and flowers, natural colorants and essential oils. Baking soda and citric acid are the essential ingredients in bath bombs. When the two combine in warm bathwater, it sets off a chemical reaction that causes the bath bomb to start rapidly fizzing. Fine sea salt, which can be found in the salt or spice section of most grocery stores, adds minerals and helps increase the fizz factor. Instead of regular white salt, you could use pink Himalayan, red Alaea or black Hawaiian salt for a different look. The oil helps moisten the bath bomb mixture without causing it to fizz too soon. Witch hazel acts as a binder to keep everything held together while it dries in the molded shape. There's a bit of a learning curve to making bath bombs, so be prepared to make a test batch or two until you get the hang of them. For best results, don't make them on a rainy or extra-humid day, and be sparing with the amount of witch hazel added to the recipe.

YIELD: 4 BATH BOMBS

1½ cups (429 g) baking soda

¾ cup (177 g) citric acid

½ cup (144 g) fine sea salt

1 to 2 add-ins (optional; see page 140)

2 tbsp (20 g) melted coconut oil or other oil, such as sunflower or olive, optionally infused with herbs or flowers

20 to 25 drops total essential oil(s) of choice

Witch hazel in a small spray bottle (optional)

½-cup (120-ml) measuring cup

Dinner plate

Wax paper, cut into 6-inch (15-cm) squares

In a medium-sized mixing bowl, stir together the baking soda, citric acid and sea salt (photo 1). If using, stir in the optional add-in(s). Mix well, working out any clumps with your fingers. In a separate bowl, combine the oil with the essential oil(s).

Slowly drizzle the melted oil into the combined dry ingredients while stirring with a whisk. Break up any remaining clumps with your hands to ensure the oil is completely incorporated.

Try squeezing a portion of the mixture into a ball shape. If it holds together without easily falling apart, it's ready to mold (photo 2). If it crumbles, spray 2 to 3 spritzes of witch hazel into the mixture while stirring, then check again. Once the mixture holds together easily without crumbling, it's ready. Be sparing with the witch hazel, as too much will cause your bath bomb to prematurely expand or fall apart.

Fill the measuring cup with the mixture, pressing firmly as you pack it in (photo 3). Turn the dinner plate upside down on your work surface. Lay a square of wax paper on top, then turn out the bath bomb from the measuring cup and onto the wax paper (photo 4). Gently slide the wax paper off the plate to the spot where you plan to let the bath bombs dry. Using the plate and wax paper in this way makes it much easier to move the bath bombs around.

Allow the bath bombs to air-dry for several hours, then wrap in airtight packaging. Be careful exiting the tub after use, as the tub floor may become slippery from the oil.

(continued)

Make Your Own Bath Bombs (continued)

OPTIONAL ADD-INS

1 tbsp (7 g) coconut milk powder–nourishes and softens skin

1 to 2 tsp (1 to 3 g) flower powders–grind to a fine powder and sift; good choices include calendula, chamomile, elderflower, lavender, rose petal or yarrow

1 tbsp (7 g) goat or cow milk powder–softens and soothes skin

1 to 2 tsp (1 to 3 g) herbal powders–grind to a fine powder and sift; good choices include chickweed, nettle, plantain, rosemary or violet leaves

1 tsp matcha green tea powder–adds a beautiful fresh green color

1 tbsp (7 g) oats–grind in a coffee grinder; soothes itchy skin

1/4 to 1/2 tsp purple Brazilian clay–adds a pretty pastel shade of purple

1/4 to 1/2 tsp rose kaolin clay–adds a lovely pink color

SAMPLE RECIPE COMBINATION IDEAS

OATMEAL ROSE BATH BOMB

1 1/2 cups (429 g) baking soda

3/4 cup (177 g) citric acid

1/2 cup (144 g) fine sea salt

1 tsp finely ground rose petals

1 tbsp (6 g) ground oats

2 tbsp (20 g) melted coconut oil

22 drops rose geranium essential oil

Topping: ground rose petals and oats

PINK GRAPEFRUIT

1 1/2 cups (429 g) baking soda

3/4 cup (177 g) citric acid

1/2 cup (144 g) fine pink Himalayan sea salt

1/4 tsp rose kaolin clay

2 tbsp (20 g) sunflower oil

25 drops pink grapefruit essential oil

Tip: If you'd like your bath bomb to have floral decorations on top, sprinkle the flower petals into the bottom of the measuring cup mold, before packing in the bath bomb mixture. Good choices include calendula flowers, cornflowers, lavender buds and rose petals. Grind them coarsely with a coffee grinder or mortar and pestle first, because smaller pieces will stick to the surface of the bath bomb best. You could also use coarse salt or coarsely ground oatmeal as a decorative topping, added in the same way as the flower petal topping.

Sore Muscle Bath Bags

Relax and ease your aches and pains with a warm bath and these aromatic salt bags. Pine, juniper and mint were chosen for their pain-relieving abilities and to complement the muscle-relaxing properties of Epsom salt and lavender essential oil. As an added bonus, the eucalyptus oil in these bath bags can also help clear stuffy noses when a cold or sinus congestion strikes!

YIELD: 3 TO 4 BATH BAGS

¾ cup (168 g) Epsom salt

4 tbsp (2 g) dried mint leaves, crumbled

¼ cup (5 g) dried pine needles, finely chopped

5 to 10 drops eucalyptus essential oil

10 to 15 drops lavender essential oil

3 to 4 reusable muslin tea bags

9 to 12 dried juniper berries (optional)

Combine the Epsom salt with the mint, pine needles and essential oils in a pint (500-ml) canning jar. Cap and shake thoroughly, until all ingredients are completely and evenly mixed together.

Divide the sore muscle salts between 3 or 4 reusable tea bags. If you don't have any on hand, you can tie up the salts in clean socks instead. Add 2 to 3 juniper berries per bag, if using, and tie closed.

Store the bags in a tightly sealed jar, to keep the aroma and essential oils from escaping.

To use, add one bath bag to the water as the tub fills, and enjoy a soothing, relaxing bath.

Tip: Gather pine needles from trees around your house and spread them out on a clean dishtowel for a day or two or until completely dry. Because they don't have high water content to begin with, they dry quite quickly. If you don't have pine trees in your area, try using a few drops of fir needle essential oil in this recipe instead.

Garden Herbs Bath Soak

This refreshing bath soak incorporates a variety of green herbs and leaves from the garden. Mix and match as you please, but choose several strong aromatics, such as mint, lavender leaves, rosemary, sage, thyme or pine needles for their energizing scents and beneficial circulation-boosting properties. If available, add a few leaves of violet or plantain to round out the mix and for their extra skin-soothing effect. Baking soda softens the water while Epsom salt helps ease sore muscle aches and pains. These bath salts are further scented with invigorating eucalyptus and peppermint essential oils to revitalize and uplift a tired spirit and body. As a bonus, these two essential oils are amazing at clearing sinuses, making this a great soak for when you have a stuffy nose or cold.

YIELD: ½ CUP (130 G) OR ENOUGH FOR 1 BATH

½ cup (about 12 g) chopped fresh green herbs and leaves, loosely packed

½ cup (112 g) Epsom salt

1 tbsp (9 g) baking soda

1 drop each of eucalyptus and peppermint essential oils mixed with ¼ tsp fractionated coconut or other oil

Reusable tea bag or a 12 x 12–inch (30 x 30–cm) square of plain muslin cloth, plus string for tying (optional)

Using a small food processor, coarsely blend the fresh leaves and Epsom salt together. Spread out the salt and herb mixture on a sheet of wax paper and allow to air dry for 1 to 2 days. The salt works to quickly pull moisture from the leaves and needles, preserving the bright green color of fresh herbs.

In a small mixing bowl, combine the dried herb salts and baking soda. Stir in the essential oils and oil mixture.

Pour into a small jar or, to make after-bath cleanup easier, tie up the bath salts in a reusable tea bag or a 12 x 12–inch (30 x 30–cm) square of plain muslin cloth.

To use, pour the loose bath salts into warm bathwater, or drop in the bag of salts while the water is running, and enjoy a rejuvenating bath. Because eucalyptus and peppermint essential oils are not recommended for use on young children, this bath is more suitable for older teens and nonpregnant adults.

Calming Bath Soak

This recipe combines two classic calming herbs—chamomile and lavender—in a soak designed to relax and soothe both body and mind. Oatmeal is fantastic at relieving all sorts of rashes and skin irritations, while Epsom salt provides magnesium that's so important for maintaining a healthy nervous system. A few drops of lavender essential oil will add an extra element of calm to your bath, but it can be omitted if you're sensitive to the stronger scent.

YIELD: 1 CUP (240 G) OR ENOUGH FOR 4 BATHS

1 tbsp (1 g) dried chamomile flowers

1 tbsp (1 g) dried lavender flowers

1 tbsp (6 g) old-fashioned rolled oats

1 cup (232 g) Epsom salt

3 to 4 drops lavender essential oil mixed with ¼ tsp fractionated coconut or other oil

Combine the dried flowers and oatmeal. Using an electric coffee grinder or mortar and pestle, grind the herbs to a fine powder.

Blend the resulting scented herbal powder into the Epsom salt, then stir in the essential oil until completely incorporated. Store in a tightly sealed jar.

Add ¼ cup (60 g) of the mixture to your tub as it fills with warm bathwater. For easier cleanup, place the bath soak in a reusable tea bag or tie up in a clean sock before use.

Calendula Spice Fizzing Bath Salts

These deliciously scented fizzing bath salts carry the subtle aroma of pumpkin spice and are perfect for adding to your tub on a cool evening in late fall or winter. Calendula flowers soothe and soften skin chafed by blustery weather, Epsom salt helps ease muscle aches, while the ginger and cinnamon gently increase circulation to warm cold fingers and toes. The fun fizzing reaction comes about when an alkaline ingredient (baking soda) comes in contact with an acidic substance (citric acid). Those with delicate skin types may find citric acid a little too intense for anything other than occasional use. If that's the case, it can be omitted. The bath salts will still work and smell wonderful, they just won't be fizzy.

YIELD: ENOUGH FOR 6 BATHS

1 cup (224 g) Epsom salt

¼ cup (56 g) baking soda

2 tbsp (24 g) citric acid

¼ tsp ground ginger

¼ tsp ground cinnamon

¼ cup (2 g) dried calendula flowers

In a small mixing bowl, combine the Epsom salt, baking soda, citric acid, ginger and cinnamon.

Using an electric coffee grinder or mortar and pestle, grind the dried calendula flowers until they're powdered very finely, sifting through a fine mesh strainer if needed. Add the calendula powder to the other ingredients.

Pour the bath salts into a reusable, shatterproof container (such as PET plastic) or an airtight bag. Seal the container. Be careful with using glass: the baking soda and citric acid combination can cause air pressure to build up inside the container over time, creating the potential for glass jars to shatter. Label and store in a cool area, out of direct heat and sunlight.

For a warm, stimulating bath, pour around ¼ cup (60 g) into your bathwater. The salts will fizz and bubble and give off a subtle pumpkin spice scent.

Be sure to avoid getting moisture in the jar and close it tightly after each use. It's imperative that fizzing bath salts stay completely dry or they will begin to clump together in the jar. If you live in an area with high humidity, you may want to leave out the citric acid and have a non-fizzing, but still lovely, bath salt. If you plan on making these for gifts, don't make them too far ahead of time as they may lose their active properties during a long period of storage.

Note that ginger and cinnamon in your bathwater will increase circulation and may promote sweating, so if you have blood pressure problems, keep the amounts low or check with a doctor before use.

Fizzy Rose Lemonade Soak

Sweet roses and zesty lemon peel combine in these fun and fizzy summery bath salts! Roses have a cooling and astringent effect on the body, making them a great addition to hot-weather recipes. Lemon peel adds a subtle, bright citrus scent while sea salt softens and rejuvenates the skin. Pink Himalayan salt lends a pretty rosy color to this soak along with an impressive 84 minerals and superior detoxification properties, but if it's not available, more sea salt can be used instead. Citric acid and baking soda combine in the bathwater to make this soak a fizzy one. If you have sensitive skin or can't find a source for it, you can omit the citric acid for a non-fizzy but still amazing bath experience.

YIELD: ENOUGH FOR 4 BATHS

¼ cup (2 g) dried rose petals

1 tbsp (1 g) dried lemon peel

½ cup (145 g) coarse sea salt

¼ cup (60 g) coarse pink Himalayan salt

¼ cup (56 g) baking soda

2 tbsp (24 g) citric acid

Using an electric coffee grinder or mortar and pestle, grind the rose petals and lemon peel together, along with 2 tablespoons (35 g) of the sea salt, until they're finely powdered.

Stir the ground mixture together with the remaining ingredients, until completely distributed throughout. Seal tightly in a reusable, shatterproof container (such as PET plastic) or an airtight bag. Be careful with using glass: the baking soda and citric acid combination can cause air pressure to build up inside the container over time, creating the potential for glass jars to shatter. Label and store in a cool area, out of direct heat and sunlight.

To use, pour around ¼ cup (60 g) into your warm bathwater. The salts will fizz and bubble and give off a fun scent of pink lemonade and summer.

Be sure to avoid getting moisture in the container and close it tightly after each use. It's imperative that fizzing bath salts stay completely dry or they will begin to clump together in the container. If you live in an area with high humidity, you may want to leave out the citric acid and have a non-fizzing, but still lovely, bath salt.

➤→ See photo on page 128.

Garden Bath Teas

Bath teas may be among the simplest of projects to make, and they're wonderfully effective and therapeutic. Essentially, you can blend almost any combination of dried herbs, flowers and spices together to make a complementary mix. Below are a few of my favorites, but feel free to mix and match the plants you have on hand to create your own personalized recipes.

Warming Ginger & Lemon Balm Bath Tea helps increase circulation and makes the perfect bath for when you feel run down or as if you're catching a cold. If larger pieces of dried grated ginger aren't available, use half as much ground ginger instead.

Lavender Sleepy Time Bath Tea combines relaxing lavender with calming chamomile and emotion-balancing rose. Take a warm bath in this tea, put on your most comfy pajamas and then settle in for a good night's sleep.

Energizing Rosemary Mint Bath Tea is perfect for those times that you need a quick pick-me-up. Rosemary increases circulation and boosts your level of alertness while mint helps awaken the mind and spirit. Juniper berries add an extra burst of energetic scent, but can be omitted if they're not easily available.

YIELD: 1 TO 2 BATH TEAS PER RECIPE

WARMING GINGER & LEMON BALM BATH TEA

2 tbsp (1 g) dried lemon balm leaves

1 tbsp (6 g) dried ginger root pieces

1 tbsp (8 g) dried lemon peel

1 to 2 reusable tea bags

1 cup (250 ml) boiling water

LAVENDER SLEEPY TIME BATH TEA

2 tbsp (2 g) dried lavender buds

1 tbsp (1 g) dried chamomile flowers

1 tbsp (1 g) dried rose petals

1 to 2 reusable tea bags

1 cup (250 ml) boiling water

ENERGIZING ROSEMARY MINT BATH TEA

1 tbsp (1 g) dried rosemary

1 tbsp (1 g) dried mint leaves

1/2 tbsp (2 g) dried juniper berries (optional)

1 reusable tea bag

1 cup (250 ml) boiling water

Crumble the herbs and flowers and place them in reusable muslin tea bags. You don't need to grind larger pieces of dried herbs such as lemon peel, ginger root or juniper berries. If you don't have muslin tea bags handy, try tying up the herbs in squares of old, white T-shirts or in clean socks.

Place the tea bag(s) in a mug or other heatproof container and pour the boiling water over. Let steep for 20 minutes, then begin running your bath. Pour the tea into the tub along with the tea bag. Making an infusion first in this manner helps the bath to be stronger and therefore more effective. If you're crunched on time, though, you can just add the tea bag directly to your tub as the warm bathwater runs in. Soak your body in the therapeutic water.

Beautiful
Bath Melts & Scrubs

Turn your bath into a mini-spa with these luxurious treats that leave your skin smooth, polished and moisturized.

Bath melts are little shapes of solid butters, such as cocoa and shea, blended with herbs, flowers and other things that are lovely for your skin. To use, drop one in the tub at the start of your bath. The warmth from the water will soften the creamy butter, melting it into the water and onto your skin, leaving behind a protective layer that helps seal moisture into your skin. There's usually no need to apply a body lotion after using a bath melt—they have a convenient and effective moisturizing system built right in!

Scrubs come in many forms and are used to exfoliate away dull, flaky skin. Because they're a rather intense skin treatment, it's best to only use body scrubs once every week or two. For tougher areas, such as your feet, you can use them more frequently until the level of smoothness you desire is reached. After that, move to a weekly or bimonthly maintenance schedule.

You'll find several fun body scrubs in this chapter plus a couple of handy scrub shapes designed specifically for smoothing rough heels and getting your feet in tip-top shape for sandal season!

Lavender Oatmeal Bath Melts

Skin-soothing oats and inflammation-fighting lavender flowers team up in this bath melt to provide relief to itchy, irritated skin. The light floral scent relaxes and calms the mind, while the cocoa butter and sweet almond oil melt into your water-warmed skin to lock in much-needed moisture.

YIELD: 10 TO 12 SMALL BATH MELTS

5 tbsp (70 g) cocoa butter

1½ tbsp (22 ml) sweet almond oil

1 tbsp (3 g) dried lavender buds

1 tbsp (7 g) oats

Combine the cocoa butter and sweet almond oil in a heatproof jar or container. Set the jar down in a saucepan containing a few inches (at least 5 cm) of water. Place the pan over a medium-low burner until the cocoa butter melts.

Meanwhile, grind the lavender buds and oats to a very fine powder using an electric coffee grinder or mortar and pestle. Sift large pieces out with a fine mesh sieve, to make after-bath cleanup time much easier.

Combine the melted cocoa butter and sweet almond oil mixture with the powdered lavender and oats. Pour into silicone molds and place in the freezer until solid.

Remove the melts from the mold and store in a cool, dry place. If your house stays really warm, you may want to store bath melts in your refrigerator or freezer.

To use, drop 1 melt into the tub while running warm bathwater. It will slowly melt in the water, leaving a fine layer of oil behind to seal in the moisture from your bath. Be careful as you exit the tub, as the oil may make it slippery. To make after-bath cleanup easier, you may want to tie up the bath melt in a clean sock or reusable tea bag before using, so that it catches any stray specks of herbs or oatmeal instead of leaving them on the surface of your tub.

Vanilla Rose Bath Melts

Pure shea butter and the heady scent of rose are featured in these luxurious melts that turn bath time into a replenishing treat for mind, body and soul.

YIELD: 12 TO 16 SMALL BATH MELTS

½ cup (110 g) shea butter

2 tbsp (1 g) dried rose petals

2-inch (5-cm) section of vanilla bean, chopped

Rose essential oil (optional)

Place the shea butter in a heatproof jar or container and set it down in a small saucepan containing a few inches (at least 5 cm) of water. Set the pan over a medium-low burner until the shea butter melts. Overheated shea butter can become grainy, so be sure to remove it promptly from the heat source as soon as it is melted.

While the shea butter is melting, grind the rose petals and chopped vanilla bean together with an electric coffee grinder or mortar and pestle, to a fine powder.

Stir the vanilla rose powder and a few drops of rose essential oil, if using, into the melted shea butter and pour into small silicone molds. Place the mold in the refrigerator or freezer until firm, then remove from the mold. It's normal for the powder to settle to the bottom of the mold (which turns out to be the top of the bath melt once it's removed from the mold).

Store bath melts in a cool, dry place or in a sealed container in your refrigerator or freezer. To use, drop in 1 bath melt as you run warm water into the tub. After your bath, as you emerge from the water, the shea butter will cling in an even layer over your skin, helping to seal in moisture. Be careful as you exit the tub, as the oil may make it slippery. To make after-bath cleanup easier, you may want to tie up the bath melt in a clean sock or reusable tea bag before using, so that it catches any stray specks of rose petals or vanilla bean instead of leaving them on the surface of your tub.

Lemon Chamomile Bath Melts

Anti-inflammatory chamomile combines with zesty lemon in these sunny melts that brighten and uplift your outlook as they soothe and seal in moisture. Lemongrass essential oil is a great choice for this recipe, adding a cheerful citrus scent for a clean and rejuvenating bath experience. Cocoa butter adds a delightful creaminess to these melts, but the unrefined version may also lend an overpowering and unwanted chocolate-like scent. If you really want the lemon fragrance to shine through, try using refined cocoa butter or substitute with barely scented kokum butter.

YIELD: 12 TO 14 BATH MELTS

2½ tbsp (35 g) cocoa butter

5 tbsp (70 g) shea butter

1 tbsp (1 g) dried chamomile flowers

1 tsp dried lemon peel or zest

Lemongrass essential oil (optional)

Add the cocoa and shea butter to a heatproof jar or container and set it down in a small saucepan containing a few inches (at least 5 cm) of water. Set the pan over a medium-low burner until the butters are completely melted, then remove from heat. Overheated shea butter can become grainy, so be sure to remove the pan promptly from the heat source as soon as the butters are melted.

While the butters are heating, use an electric coffee grinder or mortar and pestle to grind the chamomile flowers and lemon peel together until finely powdered.

Stir the chamomile-lemon powder into the melted butters. For a bright lemon scent, add a few drops of lemongrass essential oil if you'd like. Pour into small silicone molds and place in the refrigerator or freezer until firm. Unmold and store in a cool area or in a sealed container in your refrigerator or freezer.

To use, drop in 1 bath melt as you run warm water in your bath. The heat from the bath will melt the butters, leaving a fine layer on your skin after bathing, sealing in moisture. Be careful as you exit the tub, as melts can sometimes make the floor slippery. To make after-bath cleanup easier, you may want to tie up the bath melt in a clean sock or reusable tea bag before using, so that it catches any stray specks of powdered chamomile or lemon peel instead of leaving them on the surface of your tub.

Calendula Spice & Honey Cleansing Scrub

This scrub polishes skin as it cleanses, leaving behind a light silky feel. Ginger and cinnamon increase circulation and warm the body as they add a delicious scent along with the vanilla extract. Calendula was chosen for this recipe because it offers multiple beneficial properties that are helpful for repairing and maintaining skin health. Sweet almond is a nourishing oil that's suitable for most skin types, but if you're allergic to tree nuts, try using olive or sunflower in this recipe instead. Mild liquid castile soap gently lifts away dirt, while honey rejuvenates damaged skin. Use this delightful scrub once every week or two for smoother, silkier skin!

YIELD: 4 OUNCES (113 G)

¼ cup (71 g) coarse sea salt

½ tbsp (7 ml) calendula-infused sweet almond oil (see page 18 for how to infuse oil)

1 tsp raw honey

1½ tbsp (22 ml) liquid castile soap

⅛ tsp ginger

1/16 tsp cinnamon

¼ tsp pure vanilla extract

Place all of the ingredients in a small mixing bowl and stir together until completely combined. Some brands of castile soap have a stronger scent than others, so smell the mixture to determine if it needs more vanilla or spices, and add extra of those ingredients if desired.

Spoon the mixture into a 4-ounce (120-ml) jar.

For best results, apply the scrub to skin dampened by a shower or bath. Scoop out a small amount and rub over dry spots and other places on your body in need of cleansing and exfoliation. You can also use this scrub as a hand wash. Rinse well with warm running water. Be careful if using in the shower or tub, as the oil might make the floor a little slippery.

➻ See photo on page 150.

Sunflower Citrus Scrub

This scrub evokes memories of bright sunshine and happiness as it exfoliates and smooths your skin. I chose sunflowers for their cheerful, bright color and skin-conditioning properties. The recipe lends itself well to other herbs and flowers such as plantain leaves, pansies, lemon balm or rose petals. You may wish to leave the scrub unscented other than the natural scent of the herb or flower used, or use a different essential oil such as lavender or peppermint. For best color and appearance, use fresh plants to make the scrub, instead of dried.

YIELD: ¼ CUP (60 ML)

1 tbsp (1 g) fresh sunflower petals

¼ cup (65 g) sea salt

1½ to 2 tbsp (23 to 30 ml) sunflower oil

7 drops distilled lemon essential oil

5 drops sweet orange essential oil

Using a small food processor, blend the sunflower petals and sea salt together. Spread out the salt-and-flower mixture on a sheet of wax or parchment paper, and allow to air-dry for 1 to 2 days. The salt works to quickly pull moisture from the sunflowers, preserving the bright yellow color.

In a half-pint (250-ml) canning jar or bowl, combine the oil and essential oils. Start by using just 1½ tablespoons (23 ml) of oil, and only add more if the final scrub seems too dry for your preference. Add the dried sunflower salt and mix well. Cover the jar with its lid and store in a cool, dry spot.

Because they're made without water, scrubs like this one don't need a preservative; however, you must keep water out of its container to prevent it from eventually spoiling. To keep my scrubs water-free, I scoop out enough for a single use on an as-needed basis, and place it in a small, unbreakable cup that can be safely used in a shower or bath.

Dandelion Orange Fizzy Bath Melts

These sweet little bath products are a cross between a bath melt and a bath bomb. They contain lots of cocoa butter, which helps seal moisture in your skin, plus a bonus bit of fun fizz from the citric acid and baking soda. I love the cheerful combination of dandelion flowers and sweet orange essential oil, but you could use other flowers for the infused oil, such as calendula or chamomile, and other essential oil scents, such as lavender or geranium rose. Be careful exiting the tub as the melted butter can make the surface slippery.

YIELD: 6 BATH MELTS

¼ cup (45 g) cocoa butter

2 tsp (10 ml) dandelion-infused jojoba oil or your favorite oil (see page 18 for how to infuse oil)

¼ cup plus 2 tbsp (91 g) baking soda

3 tbsp (39 g) citric acid

45 drops (1.5 g) sweet orange essential oil

Place the cocoa butter and infused oil in a half-pint (250-ml) heatproof jar. Set the jar down in a small saucepan containing 1 to 2 inches (2.5 to 5 cm) of water, then place the pan over a medium-low burner until the butter has melted.

While the butter is melting, combine the baking soda and citric acid in a small mixing bowl. Mix well, breaking up any lumps you find with the back of a spoon.

Remove the melted butter-and-oil mixture from the heat. Stir in the baking soda and citric acid, then add the essential oil. Mix well, then spoon into small silicone molds. Place in the refrigerator for 2 to 3 hours until the melts are completely cool and solid. Remove from the refrigerator, and store in an airtight container or packaging in a dry, cool area.

Wildflower Shower Scrub Bars

A shower scrub bar is like a lotion bar that you use in your shower, only it has scrubby bits to help polish and exfoliate your skin. These bars also contain a small amount of emulsifying wax, so you're not left with a thick, greasy feel on your skin—just a nice layer of moisturizing softness. If you don't have emulsifying wax, you could leave it out, although the bar will leave a heavier layer of butter on your skin and may make the shower floor more slippery. Baking soda and cream of tartar add extra scrub power; sensitive skin types may find the combination too abrasive, so both ingredients can be omitted if you'd like. You can use any type of dried wildflower such as elder, dandelion, daisies, violets or yarrow. Or you might want to try garden favorites such as lavender, cornflowers or roses. The recipe is very adaptable!

YIELD: 3 (2-OUNCE [56-G]) BARS

¼ cup (45 g) cocoa butter

1½ tbsp (5 g) coconut oil, optionally infused with flowers or herbs

½ tbsp (4 g) emulsifying wax NF (optional)

3 tbsp (21 g) rolled oats

2 tbsp (2 g) dried flowers, or herbs

2 tsp (11 g) baking soda (optional)

1 tsp cream of tartar (optional)

¼ cup plus 2 tbsp (84 g) granulated sugar

8 drops lavender essential oil

8 drops sweet orange essential oil

Combine the cocoa butter, coconut oil and emulsifying wax in a half-pint (250-ml) canning jar. Set the jar down in a small saucepan containing 2 to 3 inches (5 to 7.5 cm) of water, then place the pan over a medium-low burner until the butter and wax have melted.

While the butter combination is melting, grind the oats, dried flowers, baking soda (if using) and cream of tartar (if using) together in a coffee grinder to form a fine powder. Combine with the granulated sugar and stir until completely incorporated.

Remove the melted butter mixture from the heat. Stir in the essential oils and the combination of dry ingredients. Mix well. Pour into small silicone candy molds or ice cube trays to create individual scrub bars, or into larger molds for larger bars. Place the molds in the refrigerator for 30 to 45 minutes to firm them up.

To use, rub the bar over your skin while showering, then rinse with warm water. Be careful exiting the shower as the floor could become slippery.

Tip: Use larger bars up within 1 to 2 weeks after their first use, or make them in smaller, single-serving sizes.

Peony & Orange Sugar Scrub

Fresh peony petals are used to naturally color this invigorating hand and body scrub. For best color results, use dark pink or red flowers. The granulated sugar in this scrub polishes away dull flakiness and increases blood flow to the surface of the skin. Sunflower oil is added for its ability to protect and repair damaged skin. After using this scrub, your skin will glow and feel silky and smooth!

YIELD: 4½ OUNCES (130 G)

Small handful of fresh peony petals (about 5 g)

½ cup (100 g) granulated sugar

2 to 3 tbsp (30 to 45 ml) sunflower or other light oil

3 drops sweet orange essential oil

FOR THE PEONY SUGAR

Place the peony petals and sugar in the bowl of a small food processor. Blend until an even texture and color is achieved. Spread the now-colored sugar in a single layer over a sheet of wax paper and allow it to air-dry for 1 to 2 days. Run through the food processor again, if needed, to break up any large chunks before proceeding with the recipe.

FOR THE SCRUB

Place the dried peony sugar in a small mixing bowl. Add the oil, 1 tablespoon (15 ml) at a time, stirring well after each addition. Continue adding oil until you've reached a consistency that you like. Add 3 drops of orange essential oil for scent. Stir well.

Because they're made without water, scrubs like this one don't need a preservative; however, you must keep water out of its container to prevent it from eventually spoiling. To keep my scrubs water-free, I scoop out enough for a single use on an as-needed basis, and place it in a small, unbreakable cup that can be safely used in a shower or bath.

For best results, apply the scrub to skin dampened by a shower or bath. Scoop out a small amount and rub over dry spots and other places on your body in need of exfoliation. You can also use it as a hand scrub after washing your hands. Rinse well with warm running water. Be careful if using in the shower or tub, as the oil might make the floor a little slippery.

Variation: If you don't have peonies growing near you, try pink or red rose or dianthus petals instead.

Create Your Own Scrub

Use this formula to create a variety of fun, easy-to-make scrubs! Adding a small amount of emulsifying wax to an oil-based scrub helps it rinse off more cleanly, but is completely optional, so it can be omitted if you'd like. This recipe is so easy to customize by changing up the type of herb or flower used to infuse the oil (see pages 10 to 17), and by using different essential oil combinations. I've given a few suggested combinations below, but feel free to create unique scrubs of your own!

YIELD: 3 OUNCES (89 ML)

2 tbsp (20 g) sunflower, grapeseed or your favorite oil, optionally infused with herbs or flowers

1 tbsp (15 g) coconut oil

½ tbsp (4 g) emulsifying wax NF (optional)

15 to 20 drops essential oil

¼ cup plus 2 tbsp (80 g) granulated sugar, plus more if needed

Combine the oil, coconut oil and emulsifying wax, if using, in a half-pint (250-ml) heatproof jar. Set the jar down in a saucepan containing 1 to 2 inches (2.5 to 5 cm) of water. Place the pan over a medium-low burner until the coconut oil and wax, if using, is melted. Remove from heat and let cool for about 3 minutes.

Stir in the essential oil and sugar. Mix well. Place the scrub in the refrigerator for 10 to 20 minutes to help it cool faster. Remove and stir well. If you think the scrub is too oily, stir in more sugar. If you think it's too dry, try adding more sunflower or another oil that's liquid at room temperature.

This scrub is made without water, so it doesn't need a preservative; however, you must keep water out of its container to prevent it from spoiling. To keep my scrubs water-free, I scoop out enough for a single use on an as-needed basis, and place it in a small, unbreakable cup that can be safely used in a shower or bath.

SAMPLE SCRUB COMBINATION IDEAS

LAVENDER PLANTAIN

Plantain-infused grapeseed oil + 18 drops lavender essential oil

CALENDULA ORANGE BLOSSOM

Calendula-infused sunflower oil + 19 drops sweet orange essential oil + 1 drop ylang-ylang

ROSE GARDEN

Rose petal—infused sweet almond oil + 10 drops geranium essential oil + 10 drops lavender essential oil

COFFEE MINT

¼ tsp ground coffee (added with the sugar) + 15 drops peppermint essential oil

Whipped Spearmint Scrub Butter

Spearmint adds an uplifting and invigorating aroma to this scrub, which moisturizes as it exfoliates. Grapeseed was chosen for this recipe because it's quickly absorbed and won't leave an excessively oily feeling behind. If that's not available, try sweet almond or sunflower oil instead. While this scrub can be used all over your body, it's especially nice for relieving and rejuvenating tired, achy legs and feet.

YIELD: 5½ OUNCES (156 G)

½ cup (112 g) shea, mango or avocado butter

2 tbsp (30 ml) mint-infused grapeseed oil (see page 18 for how to infuse oil)

40 to 50 drops spearmint essential oil (optional)

¼ cup (50 g) granulated sugar

Place the shea, mango or avocado butter in a medium mixing bowl. For this recipe, you don't need to melt the butter first. If the brand or type of butter that you have is excessively hard, try buying from another source. You want a slightly soft texture for this project.

Using a handheld or stand mixer, beat the butter for 2 to 3 minutes or until light and fluffy. If using an inexpensive handheld mixer, you may need to periodically stop beating while making this recipe so you won't overheat the motor. Add the mint-infused oil and spearmint essential oil, then beat for an additional 2 to 3 minutes. The butter should now be light and fluffy, much like buttercream frosting.

Lightly fold the sugar into the whipped butter until it's evenly distributed. Spoon into jars for storage.

For best results, apply the scrub to skin dampened by a shower or bath. Scoop out a small amount and rub over dry spots and other places on your body in need of exfoliation. Avoid using on the face or other sensitive areas. Rinse well with warm running water. Be careful when using in the shower or bath, as the oils from the scrub tend to make the floor a little slippery.

Because they're made without water, scrubs like this one don't need a preservative; however, you must keep water out of its container to prevent it from eventually spoiling. To keep my scrubs water-free, I scoop out enough for a single use on an as-needed basis, and place it in a small, unbreakable cup that can be safely used in a shower or bath.

Variation: For a relaxing scrub butter, try substituting spearmint with lavender instead.

Floral Salt Foot Scrub Bars

By blending salt and fresh flowers together, then binding them with skin-softening coconut oil, you can create a rainbow of these naturally colored scrub bars that polish and smooth rough, dry feet. Some flowers that work well in this recipe include violets, roses, dandelions, peonies, dianthus and forsythia. For a pretty green tint, try mint or lemon balm. While most scrubs should be used only once every week or two, if your feet are particularly rough or dry, you can use more often until the level of smoothness you desire is reached.

YIELD: 4 OR 5 SCRUB BARS

¼ cup (70 g) coarse sea salt

¼ cup (5 g) loosely packed fresh flower petals

2 tbsp (27 g) coconut oil

TO MAKE THE FLORAL SALTS

Using a small coffee grinder, blend the sea salt and flower petals together. Spread the now-colored salt onto a sheet of wax paper and allow to air-dry overnight. The salt helps to rapidly dry the fresh petals, without the fading of color that normally occurs when you dry flowers. The result is brightly colored salts that last for months and look beautiful in scrub and bath-salt recipes.

TO MAKE THE SALT SCRUB BARS

Melt the coconut oil in a small saucepan. Stir in the floral-colored salt. Scoop the mixture into shaped silicone molds and place in the freezer for half an hour, or until solid.

These melt easily in warm weather, so store in an airtight container in your refrigerator or freezer.

Use 1 or 2 bars during bath time to scrub the bottom of your feet. The salts will dissolve into the bathwater after their exfoliating job is done, while the coconut oil stays behind to seal in moisture, leaving your skin soft and smooth. Be careful as you exit the tub, as the coconut oil can make the floor slippery.

Chamomile Brown Sugar Scrub Cubes

These scrub cubes feature brown sugar, which acts as a gentle exfoliant to polish away dull, flaky skin. Chamomile was selected for this recipe because it helps calm and soothe most skin types. Coconut oil is an excellent antimicrobial and moisturizer, but if you happen to be allergic to it, you can replace it with another oil, such as sunflower, olive or sweet almond. Honey always makes a great addition to skin-care recipes because it leaves your skin feeling wonderfully rejuvenated after it's washed off. Creamy cocoa butter binds all of these ingredients together in a convenient and easy-to-use cube form that will leave your skin feeling smooth and silky.

YIELD: 5 SCRUB CUBES

2 tbsp (28 g) cocoa butter

1 1/2 tbsp (15 g) chamomile-infused coconut oil (see page 18 for how to infuse oil)

1/2 tbsp (7 ml) raw honey

1/4 cup (56 g) brown sugar

Place the cocoa butter and chamomile-infused coconut oil in a heatproof jar or, for easy cleanup, an empty, unlined soup can. Place the jar or can in a saucepan containing a few inches (7 cm) of water. Set the pan over a medium-low burner until the cocoa butter is melted.

Remove from heat and stir in the honey and brown sugar. Scoop the mixture into the sections of an ice cube tray, then place in the freezer until solid. Remove from the mold.

During summer and in warm climates, store the scrub cubes in a cool place or even your refrigerator to prevent melting.

Use 1 to 2 cubes during your shower or bath on dry, rough areas of skin that need exfoliating. These are especially effective on feet to help them get summer-sandal ready. Scrubs generally should be used only once every week or two, but if using on tough areas such as your feet, you can use them more often until you reach a level of smoothness you're happy with. Be careful as you exit the tub after using a scrub cube, as the cocoa butter and coconut oil can make the floor slippery.

Favorite Herbal Lip Balms

While I've listed a few fun lip balm recipes on the following pages, they represent only a tiny fraction of the potential recipe combinations to be created. After you've tried out one or two of my projects, flip to page 182 and try your hand at making your own custom lip balms from scratch!

The ingredients for each recipe are listed by weight. You'll get the best results by using a digital scale to measure them out. I realize, though, that some may not have access to a scale, which makes it difficult to follow the recipes closely. Here are a few volume equivalents to help you approximate the recipes more easily:

- 1 tbsp of oil = 10 to 12 grams
- 1 tbsp cosmetic butter = about 14 grams
- 1 tbsp tightly packed beeswax, grated or pastilles = about 10 grams

The directions for each lip balm are the same, so choose one that sounds good to you (pages 178 to 181), assemble the ingredients and follow the directions below.

To Make the Lip Balm or Tint

Combine the oil(s), butter (if using) and beeswax in a heatproof jar or container. For easy cleanup, you can use an empty, unlined tin can. If your recipe calls for alkanet root as a colorant, add it to the oils before heating.

Set the jar down in a saucepan that has 1 to 2 inches (2.5 to 5 cm) of water in the bottom, then place the pan over a medium-low burner until the wax is melted. Remove from heat, add essential oils, if desired, and pour into lip balm tubes or small tins.

Allow the lip balm to cool for several hours or until completely firm. Cap and store out of direct heat and sunlight. When stored properly, lip balm will stay fresh for 6 to 9 months.

Favorite Herbal Lip Balms (continued)

Classic Peppermint Lip Balm

Castor oil lends a slight glossy sheen and helps this minty fresh balm glide on smoothly, leaving lips feeling hydrated and refreshed.

YIELD: 12 TO 14 TUBES OF LIP BALM

1 oz (28 g) mint-infused sunflower oil
(see page 18 for how to infuse oil)

0.5 oz (14 g) castor oil

0.5 oz (14 g) beeswax

8 to 10 drops peppermint essential oil

Chocolate Mint Lip Balm

This lip balm has a yummy chocolate-mint flavor thanks to the addition of real chocolate chips and peppermint essential oil. Melt the chocolate chips in the same container and at the same time as you melt the beeswax and cocoa butter.

YIELD: 14 TO 16 TUBES OF LIP BALM

1.5 oz (42 g) mint-infused grapeseed oil
(see page 18 for how to infuse oil)

0.5 oz (14 g) cocoa butter

0.5 oz (14 g) beeswax

6 chocolate chips

10 to 12 drops peppermint essential oil

Basil & Lime Lip Balm

Basil is a terrific herb with anti-inflammatory and antiaging properties. Lime essential oil adds a sprightly flavor and scent, but double check that the brand you use is distilled, so that it doesn't cause your lips to be more sensitive to sun exposure.

YIELD: 12 TO 14 TUBES OF LIP BALM

1 oz (28 g) basil-infused olive oil
(see page 18 for how to infuse oil)

0.5 oz (14 g) castor oil

0.5 oz (14 g) beeswax

10 to 12 drops distilled lime essential oil

Favorite Herbal Lip Balms (continued)

Daisy Vanilla Lip Balm (1)

The common daisy has been studied and shown to have some quite remarkable healing properties. Use this balm on chapped or damaged lips. Vanilla absolute oil, which is not the same thing as vanilla extract, adds a nice bit of scent, but if you're unable to procure some, you can omit it or try another essential oil, such as peppermint.

YIELD: 14 TO 16 TUBES OF LIP BALM

1.5 oz (42 g) daisy-infused olive oil
(see page 18 for how to infuse oils)

0.5 oz (14 g) mango butter

0.5 oz (14 g) beeswax

10 to 12 drops vanilla absolute oil

Dandelion Plantain Chapped Lip Treatment (2)

Dandelion and plantain are two of the greatest skin-healing herbs around. The best part about them is that often they're available in your own yard, free for the picking! If you suffer from dry, chapped lips, try this recipe for soothing relief.

YIELD: 6 (0.5-OUNCE [14-G]) TINS

1 oz (28 g) dandelion-infused oil
(see page 18 for how to infuse oils)

1 oz (28 g) plantain-infused oil

0.5 oz (14 g) kokum butter

0.5 oz (14 g) castor oil

0.5 oz (14 g) beeswax

10 to 12 drops peppermint essential oil

Rosy Lip Tint (3)

Alkanet root provides the rosy red color in this lip balm that appears dark in the tin, but shows up as a sheer pale pink when rubbed over your lips. You can adjust the amount of alkanet root at will for lighter or darker shades of pink or red.

YIELD: 4 (0.5-OUNCE [14-G]) TINS

1.5 oz (42 g) rose-infused oil
(see page 18 for how to infuse oils)

0.5 oz (14 g) castor oil

0.5 oz (14 g) beeswax

1/8 tsp alkanet root

Vegan Sunflower Lip Tint

Sunflower wax is colorless, resulting in a pure white lip balm that takes color nicely. In keeping with the sunflower theme and because of its terrific skin-conditioning properties, I used sunflower-infused sunflower oil in this recipe.

YIELD: 2 (0.5-OUNCE [14-G]) TINS

0.65 oz (19 g) shea butter

0.15 oz (4 g) sunflower wax

0.5 oz (14 g) sunflower-infused sunflower oil
(see page 18 for how to infuse oils)

1/8 tsp alkanet root

Create Your Own Lip Balm

Homemade lip balm is so easy to make and so much better than store bought! By learning just one basic formula, you can create an almost unlimited variety of personalized lip balms and glosses. They make wonderful gifts to share with friends and family as well!

This basic formula is the cornerstone of every lip balm recipe that I make. It helps nourish and protect the delicate skin found on our lips and keeps them feeling hydrated and smooth. Be sure to read on past the recipe instructions for the helpful sections on customizing your lip balm further with herbs, essential oils, natural colorants and honey.

YIELD: 12 TO 16 TUBES OF LIP BALM

1.5 oz (43 g) oil, infused or plain (see page 18 for how to infuse oils)

0.5 oz (14 g) shea, mango or avocado butter (optional)

0.5 oz (14 g) beeswax

8 to 12 drops essential oil (optional)

Tip: If the lip balm is intended for use in jars or metal tins instead of tubes, add another ½ ounce (7 g) of oil for a softer consistency that can be applied more easily with your finger.

Variation: For a vegan option, use 8 to 10 grams of candelilla wax or 6 to 8 grams of sunflower wax instead of beeswax.

Combine your chosen oil(s), butter (if using) and beeswax in a canning jar, unlined tin can or other heatproof container.

Shea, mango or avocado butters are soft enough that you can add them to the recipe, if you'd like, without them adversely affecting the ratios of oil to wax. However, if you decide to use a hard butter such as cocoa or kokum instead, you may need to add 3 or 4 extra grams of oil to compensate for the extra firmness they bring to lip balm.

Set the jar or container down in a saucepan that has 1 to 2 inches (2.5 to 5 cm) of water in the bottom. Place the pan over a medium-low burner until the wax is melted. Remove from heat, add essential oils, if desired, and pour into lip balm tubes or small tins.

Allow the lip balm to cool for several hours or until completely firm. If you find that your lip balm is too soft, you can melt it back into a liquid state and add a little more beeswax. Conversely, if your lip balm is too firm, you can melt it again and add more oil.

Cap and store the finished product out of direct heat and sunlight. The shelf life of lip balm depends on the quality and age of the ingredients that you start with. Older oils will go rancid more quickly, but homemade lip balm usually stays fresh for 6 to 9 months.

Customizing Your Lip Balm Recipes

A FEW HERBS AND FLOWERS TO CONSIDER INFUSING IN OIL FOR USE IN YOUR LIP BALM CREATIONS

Basil—skin repairing

Calendula—healing

Chamomile—anti-inflammatory

Daisy—heals damaged skin

Dandelion Flowers—for cracked, chapped skin

Lemon Balm—fights the virus that causes cold sores

Plantain—for chapped lips

Mint—lightly scents oil

Rose—soothing

Sunflower Petals—skin conditioning

Violet Leaf—for flaky, dry lips

SOME OILS THAT DO WELL IN LIP BALM

Apricot Oil—for sensitive or mature skin

Avocado Oil—nourishing

Castor Oil—highly recommended, adds gloss and smoothness

Coconut Oil—melts easily, so counts as an oil instead of solid butter

Grapeseed Oil—light, absorbs quickly

Hemp Seed Oil—nutritious

Olive Oil—all-purpose, easy to find

Sunflower Oil—light, heals damaged skin

Sweet Almond Oil—softens lips

Tamanu Oil—helps a variety of skin conditions

While they're an optional component, cosmetic butters can enrich your recipe and help your lip balm to stay on longer. Shea, mango or avocado butter are soft enough that you can add them to the recipe, if you'd like, without them adversely affecting the ratios of oil to wax. However, if you decide to use a hard butter such as cocoa or kokum instead, you may need to add 3 or 4 extra grams of oil to compensate for the extra firmness they bring to lip balm.

SOME GOOD BUTTER CHOICES

Cocoa Butter—rich and creamy, protects skin

Kokum Butter—for dry, cracked skin, a good substitute for cocoa butter

Shea Butter—for weathered, dry skin, unrefined tends to have a distinctive smell

Mango Butter—moisturizes and softens, can be exchanged for shea butter

Avocado Butter—wonderfully smooth and nourishing, suitable for those with tree-nut allergies

(continued)

Adding Colors and Essential Oils to Lip Balms

Because lip balms contain oils and no water, they should be colored with oil-soluble colorants such as:

Alkanet Root—use a tiny pinch to get colors ranging from pink to dark red

Annatto Seed—for shades of orange

Chlorella—for a pale shade of lime green

For best results, infuse your oil with the natural colorant a few days ahead of time, then strain through a cheesecloth before using. This keeps little specks from appearing in your balm.

Colored clays are not recommended, as they may pull moisture from your lips and dry them out.

The judicious use of essential oils can add a delightful scent to your lip balm. In some ways they act as a light flavoring, too, but not like the candy-flavored lip balms you may remember from your youth. Cold-pressed lemon and lime oils are phototoxic, which means they can make you more prone to sunburn if you apply them before outdoor activities; however, distilled versions are available and are safer to use.

- Lemon (distilled only)
- Lime (distilled only)
- Mandarin
- Tangerine
- Sweet Orange
- Peppermint
- Rose
- Spearmint
- Vanilla Absolute

For a hint of chocolate, try stirring in a pinch of unsweetened cocoa powder, unrefined cocoa butter or a few chocolate chips into the melted lip balm before pouring into tubes or tins.

Adding Honey to Lip Balm

Lip balm is a naturally anhydrous product. That means it contains all oil and no water. Honey, however, is a water-based product. While we know that water and oil won't readily mix, it is possible to make a lip balm with honey, with a few caveats.

After melting your lip balm ingredients, remove from heat and stir in the honey while it's still hot. For the lip balm formula given in this book, add around ¼ teaspoon of honey. Stir continuously for about 2 minutes, then let the mixture sit until it starts to firm up. Stir again for 2 to 3 more minutes and spoon into tubes or small jars. The extra stirring will help the honey better incorporate into the lip balm, although over time, it will still tend to bead out. Don't store a honey-containing lip balm in tins, as any type of water-based ingredient could make them rust.

Chamomile Lip Scrub

Winter weather and heated indoor air can play havoc on skin, hair and lips. Use this gentle scrub, once every week or two, followed by a nourishing lip balm, to remedy dry, flaky lips. Chamomile was chosen for this recipe because of its ability to soothe and relieve irritation and inflammation. Sunflower is excellent for repairing broken skin, but other oils that work well in this recipe include olive, sweet almond, rosehip, jojoba, hemp and avocado.

YIELD: $\frac{1}{4}$ CUP (60 ML) LIP SCRUB

2 tbsp (30 ml) sunflower oil

1 tbsp (1 g) dried chamomile flowers

2 tbsp (26 g) granulated sugar

Using one of the methods on page 18, infuse the sunflower oil with the chamomile flowers. Strain the finished oil.

Combine the sugar and infused oil and stir well. Spoon into a glass jar. Store in a cool location, out of direct sunlight.

To use, rub a small amount over dry, flaky lips with your finger. Be light-handed and gentle as the skin on your lips is very thin and sensitive. Although the ingredients are technically edible and won't harm you if licked, this recipe isn't intended for consumption. Rinse the scrub off with warm water and follow with a handmade, moisturizing lip balm from earlier in the chapter.

➤→ See photo on page 174.

Winter Cold Care Lip Butter

This recipe is loaded with creamy shea butter to nourish and protect your lips from the ravages of dry winter weather. It features purple coneflower (*Echinacea purpurea*) to repair and soothe damaged skin, along with lemon balm, which has been shown to be particularly effective against the virus that causes cold sores. I used sweet almond oil to infuse the dried herbs in this recipe; other good options include sunflower, rice bran or olive oil. A small amount of beeswax thickens the mixture and adds an extra protective layer on your lips. Leave this unflavored or add an essential oil such as sweet orange or peppermint.

YIELD: 4 OUNCES (120 ML)

¼ cup (47 g) shea butter

¼ cup (46 g) purple coneflower— and lemon balm—infused oil (see page 18 for how to infuse oil)

2 tsp (6 g) beeswax pastilles

15 to 20 drops sweet orange or peppermint essential oil (optional)

Combine the butter, oil and beeswax in a half-pint (250-ml) heatproof jar or container. Set the jar down in a saucepan that has 1 to 2 inches (2.5 to 5 cm) of water in the bottom, then place the pan over a medium-low burner until the butter and wax are melted. Remove from heat.

Let the hot mixture cool for 5 minutes, then stir in the essential oil, if using. Place the lip butter in the refrigerator and chill for 20 to 30 minutes, checking and stirring every 5 minutes. Stirring frequently as it cools is key to getting a smooth, creamy balm-like texture.

Continue cooling and stirring frequently until the lip butter is completely cooled and can be spooned into small stainless steel tins or glass jars. Apply with a clean fingertip to soothe, heal and protect lips. This butter can also be used on other dry skin areas such as elbows, knees and hands.

Tip: If you find that the texture is too soft for your liking, you can remelt it and add an extra teaspoon of beeswax pastilles.

Lip Gloss Pots

These cute little pots of lip gloss are made with less beeswax than regular lip balm, and contain a generous dose of castor oil—the ingredient that makes lip balm extra shiny on your lips. Coconut oil rounds out the ingredient list; if you're allergic, you can use sunflower or sweet almond oil instead, and just add an extra ¼ teaspoon of beeswax before melting. The amount of alkanet powder used will determine the color of the lip gloss: use only a sprinkle for pale pink, or add more for a darker burgundy color, which will be very sheer and add a barely-there tint to your lips. You could also omit the alkanet powder for a clear gloss. The consistency of this gloss is on the liquid side, so when it's stored in tiny pots, it could leak out if the container gets tilted or jostled around a lot, such as if one was carried in a purse. If you want a sturdier glossy lip balm for travel or if you find the texture is too thin for your preference, melt the gloss again and add an extra pinch of beeswax.

YIELD: 4 TABLESPOONS (60 ML) LIP GLOSS

2 tbsp (25 g) castor oil

2 tbsp (18 g) coconut oil, optionally infused with calendula or other herbs (see page 18 for how to infuse oil)

1 tsp beeswax

Small pinch of alkanet root powder for color (optional)

3 or 4 drops peppermint or sweet orange essential oil

Place the castor oil, coconut oil, beeswax and alkanet powder (if using) in a half-pint (250-ml) heatproof jar or container. Set the jar down in a small saucepan containing 1 to 2 inches (2.5 to 5 cm) of water, then place the pan over a medium-low burner until the beeswax has melted.

Remove the jar from the heat and let cool for 5 minutes. Add the essential oil and mix well. Place the jar in the refrigerator to cool for 15 minutes. Remove and stir. Pour the lip gloss into small lip-pot containers or jars.

Mint Lip Scrub

This naturally colored lip scrub is a delightful way to use mint from the garden. Common white sugar is a brilliant exfoliant that works to polish away dry, flaky skin. It's paired here with nourishing sweet almond oil to help soften and condition your lips. If you're allergic to almonds or other tree nuts, try olive, sunflower or avocado oil instead. Because scrubs are intensive treatments and lips are delicate, it's best to use this scrub only once every week or two, followed by a moisturizing lip balm, for softer, smoother lips.

YIELD: 3 TABLESPOONS (37 G) LIP SCRUB

2 tbsp (26 g) granulated sugar

2 to 3 fresh mint leaves, chopped

1 tbsp (15 ml) sweet almond oil or other oil, such as sunflower or olive

Using a small food processor, blend the sugar and mint leaves until finely ground and evenly mixed. Spread out the sugar over a sheet of wax paper to dry for 1 to 2 days. The sugar will retain a fresh green color, even when dried. If needed, run the mint sugar through the food processor once more to smooth out any clumps before proceeding with the recipe.

Combine the sugar and oil together in a half-pint (250-ml) jar.

To use, rub a small amount over dry, flaky lips with your finger. Be light-handed and gentle, as the skin on your lips is very thin and sensitive. Although the ingredients are technically edible and won't harm you if licked, this recipe isn't intended for consumption. Rinse the scrub off with warm water and follow with a handmade, moisturizing lip balm from earlier in the chapter.

Tip: Mix up extra mint sugar when fresh mint is in season to use later in the year for both cosmetic and food use. Mint sugar is wonderful in tea, on toast and sprinkled on muffins!

Luscious Hair Care

Shiny, beautiful hair starts from the inside with a healthy diet and lifestyle, and it is further helped with regular trims and haircuts. In spite of our best efforts, though, daily exposure to blow-dryers, flatirons, pool water and the sun can all play havoc on our locks.

Before you drop a lot of money for expensive products to repair and care for your hair, try some of these DIY home treatments made from easy-to-find, all-natural ingredients, such as honey, coconut oil and vinegar, coupled with beneficial herbs and flowers straight from your backyard or local grocery store.

Because no one hair type or person is exactly alike, this chapter is filled with recipes that are ultra-easy to customize to your hair's unique quirks and characteristics.

You'll find customizable formulas to create herbal hair masks, shampoos and vinegar rinses, tailored specifically for the needs of your hair and scalp, plus favorite recipes I've successfully used for years, including a well-loved and easy-to-adapt detangling spray my mom used on me as a kid!

Lavender Orange Detangling Spray

This is a variation of a homemade detangling spray my mom made for my sisters and me when we were kids with messy, tangled hair and an aversion to hairbrushes. And it's one that I used with my own daughter's waist-length tresses. While my mom used water in her recipe, and I did too for many years, I now prefer using hydrosols for their added aromatherapeutic properties and benefits for your scalp. You may wish to infuse the jojoba oil first, such as in Sunflower Hot Oil Treatment (page 201). Besides sunflower, other suggested herbs and flowers for infusing the oil include rose, calendula, chamomile, rosemary, nettle or lavender. I specifically chose lavender and sweet orange essential oils because they're safe for children and have a great synergy that reduces anxiety and promotes a feeling of calm. Feel free to use your favorite essential oil and hydrosol combination for variety.

YIELD: 2 OUNCES (60 ML)

$1/2$ tsp jojoba oil

2 drops lavender essential oil

1 drop sweet orange essential oil

$1/4$ cup (60 ml) hydrosol or distilled water

In a small 2-ounce (60-ml) spray bottle, combine the jojoba oil and essential oils. Swirl the bottle a few times, so the two are mixed well. Pour the hydrosol or water into the bottle. Attach the sprayer top and shake well. Shake vigorously before each use. Shelf life is 1 to 2 weeks, if stored in the refrigerator between uses.

To use, spritz the detangler over the ends and middle strands of your hair. Comb or brush the spray through your hair to smooth out any tangles. As with all hair products, avoid spraying in your eyes.

Tip: What is a hydrosol?
Hydrosols, also called hydrolats, are aromatic waters that are created when essential oils are distilled. They carry many of the benefits associated with the essential oil, but are extra gentle. I used blood orange hydrosol in this recipe; other good choices include calendula, lavender, chamomile, neroli or lemon verbena.

Hollyhock Split-End Crème

The only true way to get rid of existing split ends is by trimming them off; however, this crème can help smooth out things between haircuts. Argan oil is well known for its remarkable properties that nourish, strengthen, protect and add shine to hair, although it's on the pricy side. If it's not in your budget, try using coconut or olive oil instead. Hollyhocks were chosen for this recipe because they smooth and moisturize, but other good choices include sunflower and nettle. Aloe vera gel makes this crème lighter and easier to wash out, while vitamin-rich shea butter helps bind everything together in a wax-free way. It's important to remember with this hair crème that you only need the tiniest bit to be effective!

YIELD: ALMOST FILLS A 2-OUNCE (60-ML) GLASS JAR

2 tbsp (30 ml) argan oil

1 tbsp (1 g) crumbled dried hollyhock leaves or flowers

1 tbsp (14 g) shea butter

1 tbsp (15 ml) aloe vera gel

2 to 3 drops of your favorite essential oil (optional)

Preservative of choice (see tip)

Infuse the argan oil with hollyhocks using one of the methods on page 18. Strain the finished oil before proceeding with the recipe.

In a half-pint (250-ml) jar or heatproof container, melt the shea butter by placing the jar or container in a small saucepan of hot water. Once melted, combine it with the hollyhock-infused oil.

Place the mixture in the refrigerator for around 30 minutes, or until it starts to firm up. Using a fork, stir well. Add the aloe, essential oil (if using) and preservative, then stir vigorously for about 2 minutes. The mixture will start to turn opaque and creamy. Set the mixture aside for 5 minutes to thicken, then stir thoroughly once more with a fork. You should now have a thickened cream.

To use, dab a very small amount on your fingertips. Working with one section of hair at a time, lightly rub the crème into just the ends. Depending on your hair type, it will take the crème anywhere from 30 minutes to several hours to soak in, leaving the tips shiny and healthy looking. If they look greasy instead, that means you used a little too much, so go lighter the next time.

Tip: For a nature-derived preservative option and shelf life of around 2 months, use 2 grams ($\frac{1}{2}$ tsp) of Leucidal SF Max to prevent bacteria plus 1 g ($\frac{1}{4}$ tsp) of AMTicide Coconut, to naturally prevent mold. For a longer shelf life of 6 to 9 months, use 0.5 g ($\frac{1}{8}$ tsp) of Optiphen Plus, which is not considered all-natural, but is paraben-free and formaldehyde-free. If you choose to omit preservatives, store the cream in the refrigerator and use within 1 week.

Herbal Hair Health Tea

This herbal hair rinse is jam-packed with herbs that promote a healthy scalp and may even help with thinning hair when used during several months. Feel free to use all of the listed herbs, or choose the ones that most appeal to you. Rosemary increases circulation and promotes hair growth. Sage fights oily scalp and is often used to gradually and gently darken gray hair. Violet leaf or marshmallow root are two great additions for soothing a dry, itchy scalp, while thyme and calendula are powerful antimicrobials that work to clear up pesky scalp conditions. Nettle and horsetail are filled with nutrients and are associated with strong, healthy hair. Make up a big batch of this tea and freeze in ice cube trays to make daily use more convenient.

YIELD: 3 CUPS (710 ML) HAIR TEA

$^1/_2$ to 1 cup (10 to 14 g) total of two or more of the following fresh or dried herbs: rosemary, sage, violet leaves, marshmallow root, thyme, calendula, nettle leaves or horsetail

3 cups (710 ml) simmering distilled water

2-ounce (60-ml) spray or squeeze bottle

Combine the herbs in a 1-quart (1-L) jar. Pour the simmering water into the jar and stir with a long-handled spoon or spatula. Depending on the type and quantity of herbs added, you may not need all of the water. Cover the jar with a saucer and let the tea infuse for 2 to 3 hours at room temperature.

Strain the tea into a clean jar. Store in the refrigerator for up to 3 days, or freeze in ice cube trays for longer storage. To thaw the tea, remove the needed number of cubes from the freezer and either place in the refrigerator overnight, or gently heat them in a small saucepan until melted.

To use, pour the tea in a small spray or squeeze bottle to make application easier. You can apply to either freshly washed or dry hair. Spritz or squeeze the tea over your scalp, trying to cover your scalp as thoroughly as possible. You may wish to do this over a basin, so you can catch any extra tea and pour it back over your scalp a second time. Brush or comb your hair as normal and let the tea air-dry. Use daily for several weeks for best results.

Sunflower Hot Oil Treatment

Instead of spending a lot of money on tiny packets of store-bought hot oil treatments, you can easily make your own at home. Sunflower petal extract is sometimes added to high-end hair-care products for its ability to condition and add shine, making sunflowers a natural choice for us to use in this recipe as well. Jojoba is an outstanding oil added for its nourishing and hair-strengthening properties, but if it's out of your price range or not available, try coconut, olive or sunflower oil instead.

YIELD: ½ CUP (120 ML)

½ cup (120 ml) jojoba oil

¼ cup (5 g) dried sunflower petals

Infuse the jojoba oil with sunflowers, using one of the methods on page 18. Strain the finished oil and proceed with the recipe.

To use, pour a small amount of infused oil into a cup or jar. Set the cup down in a bowl of very hot (but not boiling) water for 5 minutes or until the oil is warmed. Massage the warm oil into your hair, starting with the tips. If you feel you need it, you can work the oil farther up your hair. Unless your scalp is incredibly dry or flaky though, you may want to stop when you get a few inches away from your roots, to avoid excessive oiliness.

The amount you use will vary greatly depending on hair type and length, but a ballpark starting amount is ½ teaspoon of oil for short hair and 1 teaspoon for long hair. Leave on for 5 to 10 minutes, then shampoo out.

For a deeper treatment, apply the oil to your hair as directed above, then wrap it up in a towel. Leave the oil on for 30 minutes to 1 hour before shampooing out.

Infused oils, such as this sunflower hot oil treatment, have a shelf life of 9 to 12 months, when stored out of direct heat and sunlight.

Peppermint Hair Growth Spray

This spray was inspired by a study I read comparing hair growth rates between a popular drug and peppermint essential oil. The study found that a 3 percent peppermint essential oil preparation induced very thick and long hair after four weeks of topical application, which was quite interesting to read! Because of its strength, I found 2 and 3 percent cold on my scalp, so I used 1 percent peppermint essential oil in this recipe. Aloe vera gel nourishes your scalp, while castor oil is a popular natural remedy for thinning hair. The remainder of the spray is made up of witch hazel, which tones and cools the scalp. When using this spray, be sure not to get it in your eyes, mucous membranes or sensitive areas; it's not designed for eyebrows or eyelashes, nor is it intended for children or pets.

YIELD: 2 OUNCES (60 ML)

½ tsp castor oil

⅛ tsp peppermint essential oil

1 tbsp (15 ml) aloe vera gel

3 tbsp (45 ml) witch hazel

In a small 2-ounce (60-ml) spray bottle, combine the castor oil and essential oil. Swirl the bottle a few times, so the two are mixed well. Pour the aloe into the jar, using a small funnel to make it easier. Swirl the aloe and oils together for a few moments, then add the witch hazel. Attach the sprayer top and shake well. Shake vigorously before each use.

To use, spritz the spray directly on your scalp, using your fingers to part your hair and lightly massage it in. Do not let the spray go in your eyes. You can choose to leave the spray on your scalp all day or rinse it out after 5 to 10 minutes.

To learn more about the referenced study, "Peppermint Oil Promotes Hair Growth without Toxic Signs," visit ncbi.nlm.nih.gov/pmc/articles/PMC4289931.

Herbal Dry Shampoo

Dry shampoos are a great solution for those days that you wake up late or don't have time to wash your hair. The key ingredient for this recipe is arrowroot powder or cornstarch, both of which help absorb excess oil. When used alone, they can leave a light layer of white powder behind, so I've created three recipes designed for light, medium and dark hair. Each dry shampoo formula includes one or more herbal powders for their scalp benefits or for use as a subtle colorant. To make an herbal or floral powder, grind dried herbs or flowers in a coffee grinder, then sift them through a fine mesh sieve to yield a soft, silky powder. A general guideline is to grind around ¼ cup (60 g) of dried herbs to yield roughly 1 tablespoon (4 g) of powder.

The light hair tones variation incorporates powdered calendula flowers for their scalp-toning properties and to break up the stark white color of the arrowroot.

Cocoa powder adds a brown tint to the medium hair tones dry shampoo while powdered hibiscus (or red rose) flowers add a hint of red.

Dark hair types need the extra cocoa in the dark tones variation in order to help the dry shampoo blend into your hair color. I added nettle leaves, too, for their hair-strengthening benefits and darker color. As an alternative, try using ground rosemary instead.

YIELD: ½ CUP (65 G) DRY SHAMPOO

LIGHT HAIR TONES FORMULA

1 tbsp (4 g) powdered calendula flowers

½ cup (65 g) arrowroot powder

MEDIUM HAIR TONES FORMULA

3 tbsp (18 g) cocoa powder

2 tbsp (7 g) powdered hibiscus flowers or red rose petals

½ cup (65 g) arrowroot powder

DARK HAIR TONES FORMULA

2 tbsp (7 g) powdered nettle leaves

½ cup (65 g) arrowroot powder

5 tbsp (30 g) cocoa powder

Combine all of the ingredients in a bowl or jar. To use, sprinkle a small amount onto the crown of your head. Start out with just a bit, because you can always add more. Work the powder into your roots, using your fingers. Brush out with a hairbrush, until no sign of the shampoo is left.

Extra Mild Soapwort Hair Wash

This hair wash is a gentle and purely natural way to clean your hair, in lieu of traditional shampoo, thanks to the addition of soapwort herb. Soapwort (*Saponaria officinalis*) is a pretty pink wildflower that can be invasive in some areas. Its stems and roots (rhizomes) are high in natural saponins, or soapy substances, that cause it to create a mild lather when mixed with water. The final consistency of this hair wash is very thin, with a low lather, but will gently clean away dirt, pollen and other environmental contaminants from your hair when used as a rinse. Rosemary and lavender leaves add a mild herbal scent and compounds for healthy scalp and hair. If you don't have lavender leaves available, more rosemary will work in its place.

YIELD: 1 CUP (250 ML)

2 tbsp (18 g) dried soapwort root

1 cup (250 ml) distilled water

1 tbsp (2 g) fresh or dried rosemary

1 tbsp (1.5 g) fresh or dried lavender leaves or more rosemary

Place the soapwort in a small saucepan and cover with the water. Bring to a simmer, cover and reduce heat to low. Simmer for 20 minutes, then add the rosemary and lavender leaves. Turn off heat, but keep the pan covered and on the burner so the herbs can continue infusing. After 20 to 30 minutes, strain the mixture into a clean jar. Store in the refrigerator for up to 3 days, or freeze in ice cube trays for later use.

To use, wet your hair with comfortably warm water. Pour the hair wash over your scalp and hair, avoiding getting any in your eyes. Because the consistency is so thin, I find it easier to either put the wash in a spray bottle and spritz it directly on my scalp, or place it in a squeeze bottle and squirt it on. Some soapwort users prefer to pour the wash over their hair, then catch the extra in a basin, which is then re-poured over their head several times until the hair is saturated. You will probably need to experiment and see which way works best for you.

After your hair is saturated with the hair wash, use your fingers to gently massage it into your scalp for a few moments, then rinse with warm water. You may wish to follow with a vinegar rinse for added shine, but it's not necessary when using soapwort shampoo.

Create Your Own Vinegar Hair Rinse

After-shampoo vinegar rinses are an important part of using homemade shampoos and shampoo bars. They help restore pH, remove shampoo residue, soften hair and can be beneficial for flaky or irritated scalp conditions. While several types of vinegars are available and have a similar effect on the hair, apple cider vinegar is preferred because it's less processed and contains more nutrients than standard white vinegar.

Use the following formula to custom-tailor a vinegar hair rinse specifically suited to your hair type. If you don't have fresh plants on hand, you can use half as much dried instead.

YIELD: ABOUT 8 APPLICATIONS (10 CUPS [2.4 L])

2 cups (500 ml) apple cider vinegar

1 cup (15 to 20 g) coarsely chopped fresh herbs or flowers

8 cups (1.9 L) water

Infuse the vinegar and herbs for 2 weeks, then strain.

To make the hair rinse, combine $\frac{1}{4}$ cup (60 ml) of vinegar with 1 cup (250 ml) of water. Depending on your hair type, you may want to adjust the ratios of vinegar and water to make the rinse stronger or milder.

Pour the diluted rinse over your hair and scalp after shampooing. There's no need to rinse, although you can if you'd like.

For a more convenient alternative, you can fill a small spray bottle with the undiluted, infused vinegar and store it in your shower. Spritz it all over your scalp and hair after shampooing, then follow with a rinse of plain water.

Herbs and flowers to consider using in your hair rinse include:

Basil—antimicrobial

Calendula—soothes scalp

Catnip—for flaky scalp

Chamomile—reputed to lighten blond hair

Mint—increases scalp circulation

Nettle—stimulates hair growth

Roses—uplifting and soothing

Rosemary—improves scalp circulation

Sage—cleansing

Sunflower—makes hair shiny

Thyme—antiseptic

Violets—soothes and won't strip moisture

Coconut & Calendula Conditioning Rinse

Use this rinse once a week as a deep conditioning, after-shampoo treatment for your hair. It features rich and creamy coconut milk, which leaves hair moisturized and healthier looking. Honey acts as a natural nutrient-rich conditioner and is helpful for scalp irritations. While you could make this without the calendula flowers, I like to add them for their ability to relieve itchy and flaky conditions, and to maintain scalp health. Other herbs and flowers that would be nice to use in this recipe include chamomile, rosemary, sage, sunflower and nettle.

YIELD: 1 TO 2 HAIR TREATMENTS

½ cup (116 g) canned coconut milk, stirred well

¼ cup (60 ml) distilled water

2 tbsp (2 g) dried calendula flowers (optional)

1 tbsp (15 ml) honey

Combine the coconut milk, water and calendula, if using, in a small saucepan. Cover with a lid. Place the pan over a medium burner and bring to a simmer. Turn heat to low and infuse for 15 to 20 minutes.

Remove from heat and cool 10 minutes. Stir in the honey. Strain the mixture through a fine mesh sieve into a clean jar. Cover with a lid and refrigerate up to 2 days, or freeze in ice cube trays for later use.

To use, wash your hair as you normally do. After rinsing out the shampoo, stir or shake the coconut milk rinse to redistribute the ingredients, then pour over your hair and scalp. Depending on the length of your hair, you may only need half of the batch. To make application easier, try putting the rinse in a small squeeze bottle. Massage the rinse into your hair for a few moments, then rinse well with fresh water.

Those with extra-dry hair and scalp may wish to use this conditioning rinse twice a week. Oilier hair types will probably want to use more sparingly and only on the ends of hair, to avoid a greasy-looking scalp.

Thyme Flaky Scalp Spray

An itchy, flaky scalp is more than a cosmetic nuisance; it can be downright uncomfortable to live with. Antifungal thyme is a top choice for cleansing the scalp and for treating dandruff, while honey reduces flakes and helps retain moisture. Apple cider vinegar works to restore pH and leaves hair shinier and healthier looking. Use this spray after each shampoo and your scalp should show considerable improvement after a few weeks. If you don't find relief by then, investigate further; you may be reacting to an ingredient in your shampoo or something in your diet.

YIELD: ½ CUP (120 ML)

¼ cup (1 g) chopped thyme, dry or fresh

½ cup (120 ml) apple cider vinegar

1 tsp raw honey

Place the thyme and apple cider vinegar in a half-pint (250-ml) canning jar. Set it aside for at least 2 to 3 days to infuse. Strain, then stir in the honey.

Pour the thyme vinegar and honey into a spray bottle.

To use, spray on your scalp after shampooing, lifting your hair as needed in order to saturate as much area as possible. Be careful not to spray into your eyes. If you inadvertently do, just rinse them thoroughly with water for several minutes. Massage the spray into your scalp for a short bit and then rinse out with water.

Variation: If thyme isn't available, calendula, lavender, mint, rosemary and sage are other good antidandruff choices.

Make Your Own Hair Mask

This mask is superpowered with herbs and flowers that help promote strong, shiny and healthy hair. Coconut oil is an excellent treatment for damaged hair; if you're allergic, try using babassu oil instead for a similar effect. Raw honey might sound like an odd (and sticky!) ingredient to put on your hair, but it helps to gently clean and moisturize hair, leaving it frizz-free in the process.

YIELD: ABOUT 12 TO 24 APPLICATIONS, DEPENDING ON HAIR LENGTH

½ cup (100 g) unrefined coconut oil

¼ cup (3 to 6 g total) dried herbs (see below)

Raw honey, as needed

Infuse the coconut oil with one or more of the herbs and flowers from the list, using the quick method on page 19. Strain. The infused oil should be stored in a cool place out of direct sunlight in between uses. The shelf life is 9 to 12 months.

Mix up small batches of this mask, as needed, using equal parts of infused coconut oil and raw honey. Try starting with 1 teaspoon of coconut oil and 1 teaspoon of honey. Stir together until blended. Use more or less depending on your hair length, texture and level of damage.

When you first get in the shower, wet your hair thoroughly with water. Apply the mask to the ends of the hair, avoiding the scalp unless it's dry and flaky. Leave on for 5 to 10 minutes while you finish your shower. Shampoo the mask out and rinse well.

How often you use this mask is highly individualized. Some hair types may benefit from more frequent use, once or twice per week, while others may find the need to use it only once every month or two. Experiment to find the schedule that's right for you.

HERBS & FLOWERS FOR HEALTHY HAIR

Chamomile—may enhance blonde highlights

Hollyhock—moisturizing

Lavender—balances all hair types

Nettle—promotes strong healthy hair

Plantain—relieves itchy scalp

Rose petals—astringent

Rosemary—promotes hair growth

Sage—used to subtly cover gray over time

Sunflowers—conditioning

Thyme—antiseptic

Violet leaves—moisturizing

Simple Homemade Soaps

Many people are interested in making their own soap, but begin to feel intimidated or overwhelmed once they start researching the craft. I know, because I was the same way for a long time!

Once I made my first successful batch, though, I realized that the hardest part of soap making is just gathering up the bravery to actually try it. Yes, you do have to follow certain safety rules, but if you take your time and work carefully and methodically, it's not difficult.

The most rewarding part about soap making for me was being able to make my sensitive and highly allergic toddler a soap that cleared his eczema and left his rough, dry skin so smooth that his doctor was beyond impressed. That's an empowering feeling that money just can't buy.

In this chapter, I'll take beginners step-by-step through the basics of soap making. Once you're familiar with the process, try making a batch of Chamomile "Almost Castile" Soap (page 226). It's a simple recipe that requires just two oils and makes a lovely, gentle soap that's wonderful for all skin types. If you don't have chamomile on hand, don't worry, I have plenty of substitution ideas for you!

Veteran soap makers will enjoy perusing the recipes, filled with nourishing and healing bar soaps, plus two easy herbal liquid soaps you can make from scratch.

Shampoo bars are a popular item to make and give, so I've included a couple of my favorites here as well, featuring sunflowers and hollyhocks—two flowers that can help smooth hair and leave it shiny and healthy looking.

Also featured is an easy-to-make, pure coconut oil soap that works fantastic as a stain stick and laundry detergent!

Soap-Making Basics

Before you jump into the process of making soap, there are a few things to know.

In order to make soap, you need to combine a caustic substance with oils or fat. In days past, our grandmothers used potash, made from wood ashes and animal fats. The problem was that there was no way to know how strong or weak the potash was and how much fat should be used in ratio to it. The result was often a harsh bar that did well for cleaning laundry, but didn't feel so great on skin!

Today, we have one standardized chemical for making bar soap. It's called sodium hydroxide, or more commonly, lye. Because it never changes, we can use online lye calculators and figure out exactly how much we need to make a perfectly balanced bar of soap every single time.

In order to do this, it's important that all ingredients, even water and oils, are measured by weight instead of volume, as inconsistent measurements will yield unreliable results.

Some people fear that because lye is a caustic substance, some might be left over in the soap and will hurt your skin. That's an understandable concern, but it's completely untrue. Every single molecule of lye reacts with corresponding molecules of oil and they both turn into something new—soap plus glycerin. There is no lye left in a properly made bar of soap.

Store-bought soaps either contain chemical detergents or lye. Look on the label of your favorite soap. If it has the words "saponified," "sodium cocoate," "sodium tallowate" or "sodium palmitate," that's just another way of saying oils that have been reacted with sodium hydroxide, or lye.

Lye is a strong chemical that does require utmost caution and respect when handling. For safety, wear a pair of goggles, to protect your eyes from splashes, along with rubber or latex gloves and long sleeves.

Always add lye to liquids, and not the other way around, or it may have a volcano effect and make a mess. When mixing lye into water or another liquid, it gets very hot fast, and strong fumes will develop for a few moments. Don't breathe these fumes in directly. The ideal place to work is in your kitchen sink, with the window open for fresh air.

Handling lye is for grownups only. Make sure small children and pets are out of the area. Lye solutions should be clearly marked with both words and danger symbols for nonreaders.

If you get lye on your skin, rinse repeatedly with copious amounts of cool water. For large-area burns or if you get it in your eyes, rinse and seek medical attention right away.

I know that all of these safety warnings make lye sound pretty scary! Keep in mind, though, that soap is made every day by many people without incident. If you can safely handle bleach, another potentially harmful chemical, you should be able to handle lye with the same amount of competence.

Soap-Making Equipment

There are a few basic things you'll need for making soap.

Digital Scale—It's important that soap-making ingredients, especially the lye, are measured precisely in order to make a balanced bar of soap. An accurate digital scale is a must. Check at your local big-box store, near the kitchen accessories section, for a reasonably priced one.

Thermometer—A candy thermometer works well to measure the temperature of lye solution and oils. Save it just for soap making, though, and get a separate one for making candy.

Small Measuring Container—This is for measuring dry lye. Mark it clearly with the words "LYE" and a symbol for nonreaders. I use a plastic cup.

Heatproof Pitcher—Use this for mixing the lye and water together. Use stainless steel or heavy-duty plastic. Some people use heatproof glass, but over time the inside develops weaknesses that make it prone to breakage, so it's not recommended.

Soap Pot or Large Bowl—This is for mixing the entire thing together. It should be stainless steel, high-density plastic, enamel-lined or ceramic. Don't use aluminum or nonstick surfaces; they will react badly with lye.

Heatproof Mixing Utensils—Use heavy-duty plastic or silicone spoons and spatulas for mixing and scraping soap into the mold.

Rubber Gloves, Long Sleeves and Safety Goggles—Use these to keep hands, arms and eyes protected.

Stick or Immersion Blender—This shortens stirring time considerably and is highly recommended. Don't use a regular handheld mixer with beaters; it doesn't work in the same way.

Soap Molds—The soaps in this book will fit a Crafter's Choice regular loaf silicone mold 1501, or approximately a 3-pound (1.3-kg) mold.

Soap-Making Basics (continued)

Lining Molds

This is a step that can be done several ways. One method is to use two long sheets of parchment or freezer paper, one cut to the exact width of the mold and the other cut to the exact length. Lay the sheets across each other so they hang over the sides of the mold. This makes it easy to lift the finished soap out of the mold by the paper.

For a quick and easy liner, buy a bag of unscented store-brand trash bags. Make sure they're not the thinnest, flimsy kind that tears easily, but they don't have to be expensive either. Open the bag and press it to fit neatly into the bottom of the mold. You'll find that you have a lot of bag left over when you're done. You can tie it up, out of the way, or trim off the excess.

You can bypass the need for lining your mold in the first place by buying silicone molds or wooden ones with silicone liners. While they have the advantage of being nonstick, they often hold in moisture longer, so your soaps may have to sit in them a few extra days before they can be unmolded.

Unmolding & Slicing Bars of Soap

Soap often can be unmolded 24 to 48 hours after being poured into the mold. It should be completely cool and feel solid when pressed. Some silicone molds or very deep ones will hold in moisture longer, so they may take several extra days before the soap is firm enough to unmold easily. If you continually have problems with unmolding soap, try reducing the water in your recipe by 0.5 ounce (14 grams) or adding around $1^1/_2$ teaspoons (7.5 ml) of sodium lactate (a salt, naturally derived from corn or beets). Both of these techniques will help the soap harden faster.

Once your soap is firm enough, remove it from the mold and place the loaf on a sheet of parchment or wax paper. Slice evenly into bars using a soap cutter or sharp, unserrated knife. How thick you slice the bars is a personal preference, but many soap makers like to cut them 1 to $1^1/_4$ inch (2.5 to 3 cm) thick.

Adding Natural Fragrance and Color

Essential oils can be added to soap for natural fragrance, although it does take a fairly significant amount, around 2 tablespoons (30 ml) per batch, to create a noticeable, long-lasting scent. (Use half as much for a lighter scent.) If you plan on scenting your soaps with essential oils, you'll find that online vendors of soap supplies are significantly more economical than local health food stores, where tiny bottles are often expensive. Many citrus essential-oil scents fade too quickly, while other essential oils are too cost prohibitive to use in soap. Some that I've found to work well include lavender, rose geranium, peppermint, spearmint, lime, 10x (ten-fold) orange, lemongrass and eucalyptus.

To color soap naturally, try adding clays and botanicals, such as annatto seed powder (for yellow and orange), purple Brazilian clay, French green clay, rose kaolin clay and indigo powder.

Soap-Making Overview

Now that you have the basics down, you're ready to make soap! Remember that all measurements are by weight, even the water portion.

STEP 1

Assemble your ingredients and don your safety gear of gloves, goggles and long sleeves. I like to lay several sheets of wax paper over my work area, to make cleanup easier. Prepare your mold by lining it, unless it's silicone. (See page 221.)

STEP 2

Weigh out the water or herbal tea part of the recipe in a heatproof container and set it down into your kitchen sink or another spot near a source of fresh air. Weigh out the lye in a separate container.

STEP 3

Pour the lye into the water or tea and stir gently with a heatproof spatula or spoon until the lye is fully dissolved from the bottom of the container. Always add the lye to water and not the other way around, to avoid a potentially dangerous, and messy, lye-volcano. Avoid directly breathing in the strong fumes. Set the solution aside in a safe place out of the reach of children and pets, and let cool for 30 to 40 minutes. The temperature should drop to 100 to 110°F (38 to 43°C) during that time.

STEP 4

While the lye solution is cooling, weigh out the oils and butters you'll need for your recipe. Melt coconut oil and any solid butters in a double boiler before adding to the other oils in your bigger soap-making pot or mixing container. Heat the oils more, if necessary, until they're 90 to 100°F (32 to 38°C).

STEP 5

Pour the lye solution into the pot or mixing container of oils. Hand stir with an immersion blender (powered off) for 15 to 20 seconds, then turn on the immersion blender and mix the soap batter, alternating every 15 to 20 seconds or so with hand stirring to prevent the immersion blender's motor from burning out. Continue mixing until trace is reached. This could take anywhere from 2 to 10 minutes. "Trace" means that the soap batter is thick enough to leave a faint, fleeting imprint when it's drizzled across itself.

STEP 6

Once you've reached trace, you can choose to make either cold process soap or hot process soap.

(continued)

Soap-Making Overview (continued)

For Cold Process Soap (1a)

Stir in any extra ingredients, such as essential oils, oatmeal, honey and such, then pour the soap batter into the prepared mold. At this stage, the soap is still caustic, so be sure to have your gloves on while handling it. Cover the mold with a sheet of wax paper and then the mold's top or a piece of cardboard. To retain heat, tuck a quilt or towel around it. Make sure it's in an area where it won't get disturbed or knocked over, then allow it to stay in the mold for 24 to 48 hours. After that time, remove the soap from the mold and slice into bars. Let the bars cure in the open air on sheets of wax paper or a coated baking rack for at least 4 weeks before using.

For Hot Process Soap (1b–5)

Pour the soap batter into a slow cooker turned on low heat. Cover with the lid and let cook for 1 hour, checking and stirring every 15 minutes. The soap will go through many changes during the process. At times, it will rise up higher and then fall back in on itself. Parts of the soap will turn dark and gel-like. This is all normal. After 1 hour of cook time has passed, give the soap a final stir. It will have a thickened consistency reminiscent of mashed potatoes. At this stage, stir in any extras such as essential oils, oatmeal, honey and such. Spoon the cooked soap into the prepared mold. Allow it to firm up overnight, then remove from the mold and slice into bars. You can use hot process soap bars right away, although it makes a longer-lasting bar if it cures in the open air for a few weeks.

Chamomile "Almost Castile" Soap

This is a great recipe for a beginner because it only contains two oils. Traditional castile is a gentle, mild, 100 percent olive oil soap, with a low, creamy lather. By adding a small amount of castor oil to the recipe, we boost the bubbles while still retaining the mildness that makes castile perfect for those with supersensitive skin. I chose chamomile for this recipe because it calms and soothes rashes and other irritated skin conditions. If you don't have chamomile flowers or tea, try using lavender, rose, plantain, violet or calendula instead.

YIELD: 7 TO 8 BARS OF SOAP, 2.7 LBS (1.2 KG)

¼ cup (4 g) dried chamomile flowers or 2 chamomile tea bags

10 oz (283 g) simmering distilled water

3.7 oz (105 g) sodium hydroxide (lye) (5% superfat)

26 oz (737 g) chamomile-infused olive oil (see page 18 for how to infuse oils) (90%)

3 oz (85 g) castor oil (10%)

FOR THE CHAMOMILE TEA

Place the dried chamomile flowers in a pint (500-ml) heatproof jar or pitcher. Pour the simmering hot water over the flowers and let steep until the tea cools to room temperature. Strain and reserve 8½ ounces (241 g) of cooled tea for cold process soap and 10 ounces (283 g) of cooled tea for hot process soap.

FOR THE CHAMOMILE SOAP

Wearing protective gloves and eyewear, carefully stir the lye into the cooled chamomile tea. The tea will turn from light yellow to bright orange, which is a normal reaction. Set the solution aside in a safe place out of the reach of children and pets and let cool for 30 to 40 minutes. The temperature should drop to 100 to 110°F (38 to 43°C) during that time.

While the lye solution is cooling, gently heat the chamomile-infused oil until it's 90 to 100°F (32 to 38°C). Add the castor oil. Pour the warmed oils into your soap-making pot or bowl, then add the cooled lye solution.

Hand stir with an immersion blender (powered off) for 15 to 20 seconds, then turn on the immersion blender and mix the soap batter, alternating every 15 to 20 seconds or so with hand stirring to prevent the immersion blender's motor from burning out. Continue mixing until trace is reached. Because this soap is high in olive oil, it may take up to 10 minutes to reach trace. "Trace" means that the soap batter is thick enough to leave a faint, fleeting imprint when it's drizzled across itself.

(continued)

Chamomile "Almost Castile" Soap (continued)

FOR COLD PROCESS SOAP

Pour the soap into a prepared mold. Cover with a sheet of wax paper, then the mold's lid or a piece of cardboard. Tuck a towel or quilt around the mold to help it retain heat. Let it stay in the mold for 24 to 48 hours, then remove and slice into bars. Soaps that are high in olive oil take a little longer to firm up and cure than other types of soap, so these bars will give you the best result if you let them cure for at least 6 weeks before using.

FOR HOT PROCESS SOAP

Pour the soap batter into a slow cooker turned on low heat. Cover with the lid and let cook for 1 hour, checking and stirring every 15 minutes. After the final stir, spoon the cooked soap batter into a prepared mold. Allow it to firm up overnight, then remove from the mold and slice into bars. You can use the hot process soap right away, although it makes a longer-lasting bar if it cures in the open air for a few weeks.

Variation: Castor oil was chosen for this recipe because it's a great way to boost bubbles in an otherwise low-lathering soap. If you don't have a way to get castor oil, though, you can use 3 ounces (85 g) of one of the following as a direct substitute for castor, with no other changes needed: cocoa butter (hardens soap), sweet almond oil (skin nourishing) or lard (hardens soap). If you use a substitute, keep in mind that your soap will still gently clean, it just might not lather as much.

Lavender Oatmeal Soap

Calming lavender is paired with soothing oats in this classic bar that's well suited for those with dry, sensitive or itchy skin. Sweet almond oil is added for its ability to nourish skin, while coconut oil hardens the bar and contributes to lots of bubbles. Olive oil, a fantastic emollient that helps soften skin, rounds out the trio of oils in this recipe. Make sure that your oats are finely ground in this recipe or use colloidal oatmeal in its place. Its purpose in this soap is to help soften the water and to soothe itchy, inflamed skin. Lavender essential oil adds a lovely, calming scent, but it's optional. This recipe makes a wonderfully effective unscented soap, too!

YIELD: 7 TO 8 BARS, 2.6 LBS (1.2 KG)

1 tbsp (7 g) rolled oats

3.98 oz (113 g) sodium hydroxide (lye) (5% superfat)

9 oz (255 g) distilled water for cold process version (or 10.5 oz [298 g] distilled water for hot process version)

17 oz (482 g) lavender-infused olive oil (see page 18 for how to infuse oils) (60%)

8 oz (227 g) coconut oil (29%)

3 oz (85 g) sweet almond or sunflower oil (11%)

2 tbsp (24 g) lavender essential oil (optional)

Using an electric coffee grinder, grind the oats until they're finely powdered. Set aside, to add later in the recipe.

Wearing protective gloves and eyewear, carefully stir the lye into the water until completely dissolved. Set the solution aside in a safe place and let cool for 30 to 40 minutes. The temperature should drop to 100 to 110°F (38 to 43°C) during that time.

While the lye cools, weigh out the oils and gently heat them to a temperature of 90 to 100°F (32 to 38°C). Pour the warmed oils into your soap-making pot or bowl, then add the cooled lye solution.

Hand stir with an immersion blender (powered off) for about 15 to 20 seconds, then turn on the immersion blender and mix the soap batter, alternating every 15 to 20 seconds or so with hand stirring to prevent the immersion blender's motor from burning out. Continue mixing until trace is reached. This can take anywhere from 2 to 10 minutes to reach trace. "Trace" means that the soap batter is thick enough to leave a faint, fleeting imprint when it's drizzled across itself.

(continued)

Lavender Oatmeal Soap (continued)

FOR COLD PROCESS SOAP

Stir in the ground oatmeal and lavender essential oil, if using. Pour the soap batter into a prepared soap mold, covering with a sheet of wax paper and then the mold's lid or a piece of cardboard. Tuck a towel or quilt around the mold to help hold in the heat. Let the soap stay in the mold for 24 to 48 hours, then remove and slice into bars. Allow the bars to cure in the open air for at least 4 weeks before using.

FOR HOT PROCESS SOAP

Pour the soap batter into a slow cooker turned on low heat. Cover with the lid and let cook for 1 hour, checking and stirring every 15 minutes. After the hour has passed, stir in the ground oatmeal and lavender essential oil, mixed with 1 tablespoon (15 ml) of water if your soap is very thick. Stir well and then spoon the cooked soap into a prepared mold. Allow it to firm up overnight, then remove from the mold and slice into bars. You can use the hot process soap right away, although it makes a longer-lasting bar if it cures in the open air for a few weeks.

Old-Fashioned Rose Soap

This lovely soap features real roses, creamy shea butter and nourishing rosehip seed oil. Rose petal—infused olive oil softens and conditions skin, while coconut oil adds plenty of bubbles and creates a harder bar of soap. Shea butter is not only great for your skin, but it adds additional hardness to the bar. Rosehip seed oil was included for its fantastic skin-regenerating and healing properties. Rose kaolin clay contributes a natural pink color, but you can use half as much for a paler shade of pink or leave it out completely for a creamy white bar instead.

YIELD: 7 TO 8 BARS, 2.75 LBS (1.25 KG)

1 handful fresh or dried rose petals

10 oz (283 g) distilled water

4.14 oz (117 g) sodium hydroxide (lye) (6% superfat)

15 oz (425 g) rose petal—infused olive oil (see page 18 for how to infuse oils) (50%)

2 oz (57 g) castor oil (7%)

1 oz (28 g) rosehip seed oil (3%)

8 oz (227 g) coconut oil (27%)

4 oz (113 g) shea butter (13%)

2 tsp (5 g) rose kaolin clay (optional, for color)

1 tbsp (15 ml) distilled water

1 to 2 tbsp (12 to 24 g) geranium rose essential oil (optional)

FOR THE ROSE-INFUSED WATER

Place the rose petals in a pint (500-ml) heatproof jar or container. Heat the water to a simmer and pour over the petals. Allow the rose infusion to steep for 15 minutes. Make sure that your tea is fairly light, and not a dark brown color, or it may affect the color of the finished soap. Strain the rose-infused water into a heavy-duty plastic or stainless steel bowl or pitcher. Cool to room temperature or chill in your refrigerator before using in soap. Use 9.5 oz (269 g) of cooled rose tea for cold process soap and 10.5 oz (298 g) of cooled rose tea for hot process soap.

FOR THE SOAP

Wearing gloves, goggles and long sleeves, pour the lye into the cooled rose-petal infusion and carefully stir until it's fully dissolved. It may turn a dark brown color as it meets the lye, but that's okay at this point. Set the lye solution aside for 45 minutes to 1 hour, or until cooled to 100 to 110°F (38 to 43°C).

While the lye solution cools, weigh the olive, castor and rosehip seed oil and place in your soap-mixing pot or container. In a double boiler, heat the coconut oil and shea butter until melted. Pour them into the container with the olive and castor oil. This should bring the temperature to 90 to 100°F (32 to 38°C).

In a small bowl, stir together the rose kaolin clay, 1 tablespoon (15 ml) of water and essential oil, if using, until smooth. This will be added at trace (for cold process soap) or after cook time (for hot process soap).

(continued)

Old-Fashioned Rose Soap (continued)

Combine the lye solution and the oils. Hand stir with an immersion blender (powered off) for 15 to 20 seconds, then turn on the immersion blender and mix the soap batter, alternating every 15 to 20 seconds or so with hand stirring to prevent the immersion blender's motor from burning out. Continue mixing until trace is reached. This recipe will reach trace within a few minutes. "Trace" means that the soap batter is thick enough to leave a faint, fleeting imprint when it's drizzled across itself.

FOR COLD PROCESS SOAP

Thoroughly stir the clay, water and essential oil mixture into the soap. Pour the soap batter into a prepared soap mold, cover with a sheet of wax paper and then the mold's lid or a piece of cardboard. Tuck a towel or quilt around the mold to help hold in the heat. Let the soap stay in the mold for 24 to 48 hours, then remove and slice into bars. Allow the bars to cure in the open air for at least 4 weeks before using.

FOR HOT PROCESS SOAP

Pour the soap batter into a slow cooker turned on low heat. Cover with the lid and let cook for 1 hour, checking and stirring every 15 minutes. After the hour has passed, stir in the clay, water and essential oil mixture, then spoon the cooked soap into a prepared mold. Allow it to firm up overnight, then remove from the mold and slice into bars. You can use hot process soap right away, although it makes a longer-lasting bar if it cures in the open air for a few weeks.

Thyme & Witch Hazel Clear Skin Facial Bar

The skin-healing properties of raw honey, tamanu oil and antiseptic thyme combine with the astringency of witch hazel in this acne-fighting soap. Skin-softening olive oil and bubble-boosting coconut oil form the base of the recipe, while sunflower oil adds a silky lather and is great for all complexions. Castor oil promotes a better lathering experience, but if you don't have any on hand, you can substitute more olive oil instead. Tamanu oil packs a powerful punch, so only a small amount is needed for its powerful antimicrobial, anti-inflammatory and remarkable skin-regenerating benefits. Be aware that the addition of witch hazel to this soap tends to give it a slight medicinal smell. If you want to omit the witch hazel, you can do so; just increase the initial water amount by 1 ounce (28 g).

YIELD: 7 TO 8 BARS, 2.75 LBS (1.25 KG)

¼ cup (5 g) chopped fresh or 1 tbsp (3 g) dried thyme

9.5 oz (269 g) simmering hot distilled water

4.17 oz (118 g) sodium hydroxide (lye) (6% superfat)

½ oz (14 g) raw honey

1 oz (28 g) witch hazel

15 oz (425 g) olive oil (50%)

8 oz (227 g) coconut oil (27%)

4 oz (113 g) sunflower oil (13%)

2 oz (57 g) castor oil (7%)

1 oz (28 g) tamanu oil (3%)

FOR THE THYME-INFUSED WATER

Place the thyme in a pint (500-ml) heatproof jar or pitcher. Pour the simmering hot water into the jar and let it steep for 15 minutes. Make sure that your tea is fairly light, and not a dark brown color, or it may affect the color of the finished soap. Strain. Use 8 oz (227 g) of cooled thyme tea for cold process soap and 9 oz (255 g) of cooled thyme tea for hot process soap.

FOR THE SOAP

Pour the completely cooled tea into a heatproof plastic or stainless steel container. Wearing gloves, goggles and long sleeves, pour the lye into the cooled thyme-infused water and carefully stir until it's fully dissolved. It may turn a different color as it meets the lye, but that's okay at this point. Set the lye solution aside for 45 minutes to 1 hour, or until cooled to 100 to 110°F (38 to 43°C).

While the lye solution is cooling, blend the honey and witch hazel together in a small bowl and set aside. This will be added to the soap later, at trace (for cold process soap) or after cook time (for hot process soap).

Weigh out and gently heat the oils until they're 90 to 100°F (32 to 38°C).

(continued)

Thyme & Witch Hazel
Clear Skin Facial Bar (continued)

Pour the cooled lye solution into the oils. Hand stir with an immersion blender (powered off) for about 30 seconds, then turn on the immersion blender and mix the soap batter, alternating every 30 seconds or so with hand stirring to prevent the immersion blender's motor from burning out. Continue mixing until trace is reached. This recipe will usually reach trace within 3 to 5 minutes. "Trace" means that the soap batter is thick enough to leave a faint, fleeting imprint when it's drizzled across itself.

FOR COLD PROCESS SOAP

Thoroughly stir the honey and witch hazel mixture into the soap, then pour the soap batter into a prepared soap mold. Honey tends to make soap heat up more than normal, so we don't need to cover or insulate this soap. Let the soap stay in the mold for 24 to 48 hours, then remove and slice into bars. Allow the bars to cure in the open air for at least 4 weeks before using.

FOR HOT PROCESS SOAP

Pour the soap batter into a slow cooker turned on low heat. Cover with the lid and let cook for 1 hour, checking and stirring every 15 minutes. After the hour has passed, stir in the witch hazel and honey, then spoon the cooked soap into a prepared mold. Allow it to firm up overnight, then remove from the mold and slice into bars. You can use the hot process soap right away, although it makes a longer-lasting bar if it cures in the open air for a few weeks.

For best results, use this soap to wash your face nightly, followed by an antiacne toner such as Dandelion Thyme Vinegar Toner & Tonic (page 48). If needed, apply a light moisturizer such as Grapeseed & Thyme Lotion (page 116) for oily skin.

Sunflower Shampoo Bar

Shampoo bars are a popular and eco-friendly way to wash hair. They work for many hair types, but if you have hard water, you may find it difficult to completely rinse out the suds. Be sure to follow a shampoo bar wash with a vinegar hair rinse to soften your locks and prevent buildup. Sunflower petals and oil make a great addition to shampoo bars as the extract is used in some high-end products to condition hair and to add shine. Argan oil is included because of its abilities to nourish, strengthen and protect hair, but if it's out of your budget, you can use sweet almond oil or more shea butter instead. Olive oil nourishes and conditions, while coconut oil hardens soap and adds plenty of bubbles. Shea butter moisturizes hair and the scalp and also helps harden the bar. Small amounts of castor oil are often added to soap recipes to help stabilize lather, but in the case of shampoo bars, a higher amount is used and is almost essential for a great shampooing experience.

YIELD: 7 TO 8 BARS, 2.6 LBS (1.2 KG)

4.01 oz (113 g) sodium hydroxide (lye) (6% superfat)

9 oz (255 g) distilled water for cold process version (or 10 oz [283 g] distilled water for hot process version)

8 oz (227 g) coconut oil (28%)

2 oz (57 g) shea butter (7%)

10 oz (283 g) sunflower-infused olive oil (see page 18 for how to infuse oils) (34%)

4 oz (113 g) castor oil (14%)

4 oz (113 g) sunflower oil (14%)

1 oz (28 g) argan oil (3%)

2 tbsp (24 g) lemongrass essential oil (optional)

Wearing protective gloves and eyewear, carefully stir the lye into the water until completely dissolved. Set the solution aside in a safe place and let cool for 30 to 40 minutes. The temperature should drop to 100 to 110°F (38 to 43°C) during that time.

While the lye cools, weigh out the oils and gently heat them to a temperature of around 90 to 100°F (32 to 38°C). Pour the warmed oils into your soap-making pot or bowl, then add the cooled lye solution.

Hand stir with an immersion blender (powered off) for 15 to 20 seconds, then turn on the immersion blender and mix the soap batter, alternating every 15 to 20 seconds or so with hand stirring to prevent the immersion blender's motor from burning out. Continue mixing until trace is reached. This can take anywhere from 2 to 10 minutes to reach trace. "Trace" means that the soap batter is thick enough to leave a faint, fleeting imprint when it's drizzled across itself.

(continued)

Hollyhock Shampoo Bar (continued)

FOR COLD PROCESS SOAP

Stir in the essential oil, if using, then pour the soap into a prepared mold. Let it stay in the mold for 24 to 48 hours, then remove and slice into bars. Let the bars cure in the open air for at least 4 weeks before using.

FOR HOT PROCESS SOAP

Pour the soap batter into a slow cooker turned on low heat. Cover with the lid and let cook for 1 hour, checking and stirring every 15 minutes. After the hour has passed, stir in the lavender and litsea cubeba essential oils, if using, then spoon the cooked soap into a prepared mold. Allow it to firm up overnight, then remove from the mold and slice into bars. You can use the hot process soap right away, although it makes a longer-lasting bar if it cures in the open air for a few weeks.

To use a shampoo bar, just wet your hair with water and then gently rub the bar over it, massaging the lather onto your scalp and to the ends of your hair with your fingers. For long hair, you may want to work up a lather with your hands first and then rub it through your hair, to avoid tangles. Rinse well, follow with a diluted vinegar rinse and enjoy beautiful, shiny hair all day long!

Dandelion Scrub Bar

A scattering of poppy seeds dots this brightly scented soap, giving texture and a gentle exfoliating effect. Dandelion flowers, which are wonderful for treating rough, dry skin, are infused into skin-softening olive oil, then combined with bubbly coconut and nourishing sunflower oil. This bar is perfect for scrubbing away dirt and grime from hands, making it a wonderful gift for the gardener or farmer in your life! It can also be used as an all-over body bar.

YIELD: 7 TO 8 BARS, 2.7 LBS (1.2 KG)

4.19 oz (119 g) sodium hydroxide (lye) (6% superfat)

9 oz (255 g) distilled water for cold process version (or 10 oz [283 g] distilled water for hot process version)

16 oz (454 g) dandelion-infused olive oil (see page 18 for how to infuse oil) (53%)

3 oz (85 g) sunflower oil (10%)

8 oz (227 g) coconut oil (27%)

3 oz (85 g) cocoa butter (10%)

2 tbsp (24 g) lemongrass essential oil

½ tbsp (5 g) poppy seeds

For smoother, cleaner skin, use daily and follow with a light but effective moisturizer, such as Basic Calendula Lotion (page 111).

Wearing protective gloves and eyewear, carefully stir the lye into the water in a heatproof plastic or stainless steel container until completely dissolved. Set the mixture aside for 30 to 40 minutes, or until the temperature is 100 to 110°F (38 to 43°C).

While the lye solution cools, weigh out the dandelion-infused olive oil and sunflower oil and pour them into your soap-making pot or bowl. In a double boiler, heat the coconut oil and cocoa butter on low until completely melted. Pour the melted butter combination into the other oils and check the temperature. If needed, heat the oils to around 90 to 100°F (32 to 38°C).

Pour the lye solution into the warmed oils. Hand stir with an immersion blender (powered off) for 15 to 20 seconds, then turn on the immersion blender and mix the soap batter, alternating every 15 to 20 seconds or so with hand stirring to prevent the immersion blender's motor from burning out. Continue mixing until trace is reached. This can take anywhere from 2 to 10 minutes. "Trace" means that the soap batter is thick enough to leave a faint, fleeting imprint when it's drizzled across itself.

FOR COLD PROCESS SOAP

Add the lemongrass essential oil and poppy seeds, then stir until they're fully incorporated. Pour the soap into a prepared mold. Let it stay in the mold for 24 to 48 hours, then remove and slice into bars. Let the bars cure in the open air for at least 4 weeks before using.

FOR HOT PROCESS SOAP

Pour the soap batter into a slow cooker turned on low heat. Cover with the lid and let cook for 1 hour, checking and stirring every 15 minutes. After the hour has passed, stir in the poppy seeds and lemongrass essential oil, then spoon the cooked soap into a prepared mold. Allow it to firm up overnight, then remove from the mold and slice into bars. You can use the hot process soap right away, although it makes a longer-lasting bar if it cures in the open air for a few weeks.

Carrot & Calendula Soap

This delightful soap is a treat for all skin types. Carrots are a nutritional powerhouse full of antioxidants and vitamin A, while calendula-infused olive oil soothes and softens skin. Coconut oil helps make soap bubbly and hard, while sunflower oil nourishes all skin types. Castor oil is a great addition to soap as it helps boost and stabilize lather. Raw honey adds a little something extra special to the bar, but if you're vegan, it can be omitted. Carrot soap is popular for use as a facial bar, but can also be used to wash your body for softer, smoother skin.

YIELD: 7 TO 8 BARS, 2.7 LBS (1.2 KG)

6 oz (198 g) bottled or home-pressed 100% carrot juice

3 oz (57 g) distilled water for cold process version (or 4 oz [113 g] for hot process version)

4.2 oz (120 g) sodium hydroxide (lye) (5% superfat)

15 oz (425 g) calendula-infused olive oil (see page 18 for how to infuse oil) (50%)

8 oz (227 g) coconut oil (27%)

4.5 oz (128 g) sunflower oil (15%)

2.5 oz (71 g) castor oil (8%)

1 tbsp (21 g) raw honey (optional)

1 tbsp (15 ml) distilled water for hot process version

Place the carrot juice and water in a heatproof plastic or stainless steel pitcher. Wearing protective gloves and eyewear, slowly stir the lye into the diluted juice until fully dissolved. The mixture will probably be a bright shade of orange and may smell unpleasant during this phase—this is normal. Set the mixture aside for 30 to 40 minutes, or until the temperature is 100 to 110°F (38 to 43°C).

While the lye solution cools, weigh out the oils and pour them into your soap-making pot or bowl. Gently heat them to 90 to 100°F (32 to 38°C).

Pour the lye and carrot juice solution into the warm oils. Hand stir with an immersion blender (powered off) for 15 to 20 seconds, then turn on the immersion blender and mix the soap batter, alternating every 15 to 20 seconds or so with hand stirring to prevent the immersion blender's motor from burning out. Continue mixing until trace is reached. This can take anywhere from 2 to 10 minutes. "Trace" means that the soap batter is thick enough to leave a faint, fleeting imprint when it's drizzled across itself.

FOR COLD PROCESS SOAP

Add the honey, if using, and stir one more time until it's fully incorporated. The soap will still be a dark or medium orange at this point, but will lighten as it cures. Pour the soap into a prepared mold. Because it has honey and juice in it, it may tend to heat up faster than other soaps, so you don't need to cover the mold. If you see a crack developing in the top, it means the soap is getting too hot. Move it to a cooler room or even your refrigerator for 2 to 3 hours to cool it down. Let it stay in the mold for 2 to 3 days, then remove and slice into bars. Let the bars cure in the open air for around 4 weeks before using.

FOR HOT PROCESS SOAP

Pour the soap batter into a slow cooker turned on low heat. Cover with the lid and let cook for 1 hour, checking and stirring every 15 minutes. Stir the honey and water together until completely blended. The extra water will help the honey stir into the hot soap, with a reduced chance of scorching. After the hour has passed, stir in the diluted honey, then spoon the cooked soap into a prepared mold. Allow it to firm up overnight, then remove from the mold and slice into bars. You can use the hot process soap right away, although it makes a longer-lasting bar if it cures in the open air for a few weeks.

Cucumber Mint Soap

Cool and creamy, this soap is a refreshing treat on a hot summer day. The French green clay not only gives each bar a pretty color, but also helps soothe itchy skin caused by bug bites or heat rash. Mint-infused olive oil conditions skin, while coconut and castor oil add a bubbly lather. Extra nourishing avocado oil is loaded with essential fatty acids to help promote beautiful skin. Perky peppermint, with its cooling, anti-inflammatory properties, makes the perfect companion for cucumber, an astringent skin toner in its own right. The essential oil also adds a wonderful scent and feel, making bath time with this soap an energizing and uplifting experience!

YIELD: 7 TO 8 BARS, 2.7 LBS (1.2 KG)

¼ of a fresh, unpeeled cucumber (approximately 2 to 3 oz [55 to 85 g])

9 to 10 oz (255 to 283 g) cold distilled water, divided

4.17 oz (118 g) sodium hydroxide (lye) (6% superfat)

17 oz (482 g) mint-infused olive oil (see page 18 for how to infuse oil) (56%)

8 oz (227 g) coconut oil (27%)

3 oz (85 g) avocado oil (10%)

2 oz (57 g) castor oil (7%)

2 tbsp (24 g) peppermint essential oil

½ tbsp (8 g) French green clay

1 tbsp (15 ml) distilled water

Purée the cucumber and about 4 ounces (120 ml) of water together in a food processor or blender. Strain the resulting liquid with a fine mesh sieve or strainer so there are no pieces of cucumber left; you'll only need the juice from it. Add additional cold distilled water, as needed, until you have 9 ounces (255 g) of cucumber and water slurry for cold process soap, or 10 ounces (283 g) for the hot process version.

Place the mixture in a heatproof plastic or stainless steel pitcher. Wearing protective gloves and eyewear, slowly stir the lye into the cucumber water until it's fully dissolved. Set the mixture aside for 30 to 40 minutes, or until the temperature is 100 to 110°F (38 to 43°C).

While the lye solution cools, weigh out the oils and pour into your soap-making pot or bowl. Gently heat them to 90 to 100°F (32 to 38°C).

In a small bowl, stir together the essential oil, clay and water to make a thick paste that will be added later in the recipe.

Pour the lye and cucumber water solution into the warm oils. Hand stir with an immersion blender (powered off) for 15 to 20 seconds, then turn on the immersion blender and mix the soap batter, alternating every 15 to 20 seconds or so with hand stirring to prevent the immersion blender's motor from burning out. Continue mixing until trace is reached. This can take anywhere from 2 to 10 minutes. "Trace" means that the soap batter is thick enough to leave a faint, fleeting imprint when drizzled across itself.

FOR COLD PROCESS SOAP

Add the combined essential oil, clay and water, then stir one more time until they're fully incorporated. Pour the soap into a prepared soap mold. Cover with a sheet of wax paper and then the mold top, if it has one, or a piece of cardboard. Tuck a towel or blanket around the mold, to help keep in the heat. Let the soap stay in the mold for 24 to 48 hours, then unmold and turn the soap loaf out on a sheet of wax paper. Cut the soap into bars and cure in the open air for around 4 weeks before using.

FOR HOT PROCESS SOAP

Pour the soap batter into a slow cooker turned on low heat. Cover with the lid and let cook for 1 hour, checking and stirring every 15 minutes. After the hour has passed, stir in the combined essential oil, clay and water, then spoon the cooked soap into a prepared mold. Allow it to firm up overnight, then remove from the mold and slice into bars. You can use the hot process soap right away, although it makes a longer-lasting bar if it cures in the open air for a few weeks.

➵ See photo on page 216.

Coconut Laundry Soap & Stain Stick

This pure coconut oil soap is intended for laundry purposes only. It has no extra oils or fats in it, making it better suited for cleaning tough stains on clothes rather than your skin. It can be used as a stain stick, as detailed below, or to turn it into a homemade Lavender Laundry Detergent recipe, see page 306. I often leave laundry soap plain, but you can add essential oils for natural fragrance if you'd like. Lavender, peppermint or lemongrass are three fresh, clean scents you may want to consider. Because pure coconut oil sets up so quickly and can be employed for laundry use after only two weeks of cure time, I prefer to make this soap using the cold process method only.

YIELD: 7 TO 8 BARS, 2.7 LBS (1.2 KG)

10 oz (283 g) water

5.15 oz (146 g) sodium hydroxide (lye)

28 oz (794 g) coconut oil

2 tbsp (30 ml) essential oil, for scent (optional)

Place the water in a heatproof plastic or stainless steel pitcher. Wearing protective gloves and eyewear, slowly stir the lye into the water until fully dissolved. Set the mixture aside for 30 to 40 minutes, or until the temperature is 100 to 110°F (38 to 43°C).

While the lye solution cools, warm the coconut oil until it's melted and 90 to 100°F (32 to 38°C). Pour it into your soap-making pot or bowl.

Pour the lye solution into the warm coconut oil and stir by hand for 1 to 2 minutes. Most often, coconut oil soap will set up quickly and you may not need to use your immersion blender. If it doesn't start to thicken after that amount of time, use your immersion blender in intermittent bursts for another 1 to 2 minutes, or until trace is reached.

Pour the soap into a prepared mold. Leave the mold uncovered and let it sit undisturbed for 2 to 3 hours. You want to cut coconut oil soap much sooner than other types of soap, as it hardens quickly and will be crumbly and difficult to cut if you wait too long. After 2 hours, check to see if the soap is firm enough to slice into bars. Even though it becomes solid sooner than other soaps, it may still be caustic for another 12 to 24 hours, so make sure you're wearing your gloves for this step.

Set the bars on sheets of wax paper or coated cooling racks and allow to cure in the open air for around 2 weeks before using.

To use as a stain stick, cut each bar of soap into halves or thirds to make easy-to-hold, stick-shaped pieces. Wet the soiled area with plain water and rub the soap directly into it until a lather forms. Launder as usual. These stain sticks should work on most types of machine-washable clothing, but always test a small spot first, to be sure.

Charcoal & Tea Tree Soap

This soap features charcoal powder for its deep cleansing and detoxifying powers, plus tea tree and lavender essential oils for their fresh scent and skin-clearing abilities. It's gentle enough for most skin types to use as a facial soap or it also could be used as an all-over body bar. A small amount of tamanu or neem oil is especially helpful for acne-prone or troubled skin conditions but can be substituted with more olive oil if needed. For extra benefits, you may wish to first infuse the olive oil with skin-loving herbs and flowers such as plantain, violet leaves or calendula.

YIELD: 7 TO 8 BARS, 2.5 LBS (1.1 KG)

3.9 oz (111 g) sodium hydroxide (lye) (5% superfat)

7.8 oz (221 g) distilled water for cold process version (or 9 oz [255 g] distilled water for hot process version)

11 oz (312 g) olive oil, optionally infused with herbs or flowers (see page 18 for how to infuse oil) (39%)

4 oz (113 g) sweet almond (or sunflower) oil (14%)

2 oz (57 g) castor oil (7%)

1.5 oz (43 g) tamanu, neem or more olive oil (5%)

6 oz (170 g) coconut oil (22%)

3.5 oz (99 g) cocoa butter (or tallow) (13%)

2 tsp (3 g) activated charcoal powder

2 tsp (8 g) tea tree essential oil

1½ tsp (6 g) lavender essential oil

Wearing protective gloves and eyewear, carefully stir the lye into the water in a heatproof plastic or stainless steel container until completely dissolved. Set the mixture aside for 30 to 40 minutes, or until the temperature is 100 to 110°F (38 to 43°C).

While the lye solution cools, weigh out the olive, sweet almond, castor and tamanu oils and pour them into your soap-making pot or bowl. In a double boiler, heat the coconut oil and cocoa butter on low until completely melted. Pour the melted butter combination into the other oils and check the temperature. If needed, heat the oils to 90 to 100°F (32 to 38°C).

Using your immersion blender, briefly blend the charcoal powder into the warmed oils. Then pour the lye solution into the warmed oils. Hand stir with an immersion blender (powered off) for 15 to 20 seconds, then turn the immersion blender on and mix the soap batter, alternating every 15 to 20 seconds or so with hand stirring to prevent the immersion blender's motor from burning out. Continue mixing until trace is reached. This can take anywhere from 2 to 10 minutes.

FOR COLD PROCESS SOAP

Add the essential oils, then stir until they're fully incorporated. Pour the soap into a prepared mold. Let it stay in the mold for 24 to 48 hours, then remove and slice into bars. Let the bars cure for at least 4 weeks before using.

FOR HOT PROCESS SOAP

Pour the soap batter into a slow cooker turned on low heat. Cover with the lid and let cook for 1 hour, checking and stirring every 15 minutes. After the hour has passed, stir in the essential oils, then spoon the cooked soap into a prepared mold. Allow it to firm up overnight, then remove and slice into bars. While you can use hot process soap right away, it will make a better longer-lasting bar if cured for several weeks first.

Herbal Home Remedies

This is the chapter where your flowers and herbs can really shine!

Here, you'll learn how to make remedies and potions for treating pains, coughs, sore throats and other such maladies. I share several of the time-tested recipes that I use to keep my family healthy and well.

It's a joy to spend time outdoors when the weather is warm and sunny, but bee stings and bug bites can put a real damper on the fun. Try whipping up a batch of Bug Bite Powder (page 261) or portable Lavender Bug Bite Sticks (page 258) for a dose of quick relief. To help keep bugs away in the first place, try mixing together some Catnip & Basil Insect Repellant Spray (page 257).

Working and playing outdoors all day can leave you with sore muscles in need of serious relief. Dandelion oil is fantastic and just what you need to ease away aches and pains. You can use it to make a handy, roll-on Lavender Dandelion Pain Relief Oil (page 268) or a quick-acting Dandelion Magnesium Lotion (page 283), which has helped many friends and family members who suffer from nighttime leg cramps.

When fall and winter roll around, colds and flu aren't far behind. Keep a stash of remedies on hand, such as Bee Balm & Lemon Cough Syrup (page 272) or Cold Care Shower Steamers (page 280), to speed up recovery time and to help your loved ones feel better fast!

Catnip & Basil Insect Repellant Spray

This homemade bug spray features catnip, for its reported ability to repel mosquitoes just as well as DEET, and basil, which contains compounds that repel flies, mosquitoes and other pesky critters. To make this spray most effective, be sure to add at least one of the essential oils listed. According to current aromatherapy guidelines, basil, citronella and lemongrass essential oils should not be used on children under the age of 2 and eucalyptus should be reserved for those who are 10 or older.

YIELD: 1 CUP (250 ML)

½ cup (10 g) fresh catnip and basil leaves, chopped

1 cup (250 ml) witch hazel

Citronella, basil, lemongrass and/or lemon eucalyptus essential oils

Water for diluting

FOR THE HERB-INFUSED WITCH HAZEL

Place the catnip and basil leaves in a pint (500-ml) jar. Pour the witch hazel over the herbs. You may need to add a little extra witch hazel to ensure that the herbs are completely covered. Cap the jar and tuck it away in a dark cabinet for 1 week, then remove and strain. The finished infused witch hazel should stay fresh at least 9 months to 1 year.

FOR THE BUG SPRAY

Fill a small 2-ounce (60-ml) glass spray bottle a little more than halfway with the infused witch hazel. Add 3 or 4 drops total of your favorite bug-repelling essential oils, such as citronella, basil, lemongrass or lemon. Fill the rest of the bottle with plain water, cap and shake.

Shake frequently before and during use, to make sure the essential oils stay dispersed throughout the spray. Spritz lightly on your arms, legs and other areas you'd like to keep bug free. If gnats are a problem while you work outdoors, spritz the brim and inside of your hat to keep them away. If you're pregnant, nursing or have other health concerns, check with a doctor before using the listed essential oils.

Depending on your body chemistry and the level of bugs in the area, this spray should help for anywhere from 30 minutes to 2 hours. Reapply as needed.

Variation: Lemon balm, lavender and mint are other effective, natural bug-repelling herbs that can be substituted for catnip or basil, if needed.

Lavender Bug Bite Sticks

These all-natural bug bite sticks are perfect for outdoor enthusiasts on the go. Lavender is a well-loved and gentle herb that helps soothe the itchiness and discomfort that minor bug bites can bring. As a bonus, it also acts as a mild insect repellant, helping to reduce the chance of new bites. I like to use sunflower oil in this recipe, as it's suitable for all skin types and has been shown to be an effective healer of broken or damaged skin, but you can use another light oil, such as olive or sweet almond, instead.

YIELD: 7 TO 8 (0.15 OZ [4 G]) TUBES

½ cup (120 ml) sunflower oil

¼ cup (9 g) dried lavender flowers

1 tbsp (9 g) tightly packed beeswax, grated or pastilles

Few drops of lavender essential oil

Infuse the sunflower oil with lavender flowers, using one of the methods on page 18. Strain.

In a heatproof jar or container, combine 3 tablespoons (45 ml) of lavender-infused oil with the beeswax. Set the jar down in a saucepan containing 1 to 2 inches (2.5 to 5 cm) of water, forming a makeshift double boiler. Place the pan over a medium-low burner until the wax is melted. Stir in the lavender essential oil, then pour into lip balm tubes.

Depending on the weather and how you measured your beeswax, you may find that the consistency is too soft or too firm. If that happens, just melt the ingredients again and add more beeswax (for a firmer product) or oil (for a softer one).

Dab on bee stings, bug bites and other itchy spots as needed.

Bug Bite Powder

This is a favorite home remedy that my children use all the time. I made it to mimic an expensive product that I had bought in the past and loved, until I realized that it was not much more than kaolin clay that could easily be bought for just a few dollars per pound. I combine the clay with finely ground calendula, an herb useful for taming inflamed and irritated skin, to create a powder that's perfect for dabbing on bug bites, bee stings, acne and other minor skin irritations. It's a bit messier to apply than the Lavender Bug Bite Sticks (page 258), but makes up for it in effectiveness!

YIELD: 1½ TABLESPOONS (6 G)

¼ cup (2 g) dried calendula flowers and petals

1 tbsp (5 g) kaolin clay

Grind the calendula flowers in an electric coffee grinder or mortar and pestle. Rub the resulting powder through a fine mesh sieve. Return the larger pieces to the coffee grinder once more, then rub through the sieve again. This should result in an extremely fine, silky powder.

Mix with the kaolin clay and store in a glass jar. Kaolin clay has a long shelf life, but because of the dried calendula portion, this powder will be at its best if used up within 1 year.

To use, dab on bug bites or other skin irritations. One application may be all you need, but if the itching or discomfort returns, apply again as needed. You can also mix a small pinch with a few drops of water or witch hazel to make a paste.

Calamine Rose Lotion

The sight of calamine lotion reminds many people of childhood cases of chicken pox, poison ivy rashes or other miserably itchy skin ailments! Make your own economical version of the effective classic, minus the extra additives. Rose petals are used in this recipe for their astringent and skin-soothing properties. If fresh roses aren't on hand, try using half as many dried petals instead. Witch hazel cools and reduces inflammation, baking soda eases itching and white kaolin clay binds up irritants while helping to soothe skin. Rose kaolin clay essentially works in the same way as the white version and can be added to this recipe in order to obtain the classic pink color of traditional calamine.

YIELD: 4 OUNCES (120 ML)

½ cup (5 g) fresh rose petals

1 cup (250 ml) witch hazel

¼ cup (24 g) white kaolin clay

1 tbsp (6 g) rose kaolin clay (optional, for color)

¼ cup (62 g) baking soda

FOR THE ROSE-INFUSED WITCH HAZEL

Place the rose petals in a pint (500-ml) jar and cover with the witch hazel. Cap and tuck away in a dark cabinet for around 1 week. If using pink or red roses, the witch hazel should take on a shade of the same color. Strain. The finished witch hazel should stay fresh for 6 to 9 months, when stored in a cool, dark location, although the color will fade over time.

Reserve ¼ cup (60 ml) for this recipe.

FOR THE CALAMINE ROSE LOTION

Combine the white kaolin clay, rose kaolin clay (if using) and baking soda in a half-pint (250-ml) canning jar. Pour the reserved rose-infused witch hazel into the jar. Stir well. Avoid shaking the jar, as the liquid will splash up on the sides and it will dry out more easily. While calamine has the word "lotion" in its name, it's not actually lotion-like. The texture is more like a thick, chalky liquid.

Seal tightly and store in a cool place. Because it contains witch hazel instead of water, your calamine lotion should remain fresh for 1 month. If it starts to dry out, simply stir in more witch hazel.

To use, dip a cotton ball or swab into the lotion and dab on itchy spots, rashes and other skin irritations. Allow the calamine lotion to dry on your skin.

➢→   See photo on page 254.

Lemongrass Cream Deodorant

This wonderful deodorant recipe was developed and shared with me by my friend Kay, who graciously agreed to let me share it with you. I did a tiny bit of tweaking and added some germ-busting lemongrass to the mix, but you could also use lavender or mint. I've tried a lot of homemade deodorants, and this is one of my favorites! You only need to rub a tiny dab under each arm for it to be effective.

YIELD: 4 OUNCES (120 ML)

2 tbsp (1 g) dried lemongrass or lemon balm, crumbled

¼ cup (54 g) coconut oil

1 oz (28 g) beeswax

1 oz (28 g) shea butter

1 tsp (5 ml) sunflower oil

1 tbsp (14 g) baking soda

1 tbsp (14 g) arrowroot powder

¼ tsp lemongrass essential oil

Infuse the lemongrass and coconut oil, using one of the methods on page 18. Strain. Place the beeswax, shea butter, sunflower oil and infused coconut oil in a half-pint (250-ml) heatproof jar. Set the jar down in a saucepan containing 1 to 2 inches (2.5 to 5 cm) of water and heat over a medium-low burner until the wax is melted. Remove from heat.

Stir in the baking soda, arrowroot and lemongrass essential oil. Stir frequently during the next 5 to 10 minutes as the mixture cools. It will turn thick and creamy. Spoon the finished deodorant into a jar. The texture will stay soft and spreadable, so it won't be quite firm enough to pour in a traditional deodorant container.

To use, scoop a small amount (about ¹/₁₆ teaspoon) out of the jar, using the tip of your finger, and gently rub it into your underarm area. Repeat the process under your other arm. Depending on body chemistry and environment, you may find that you only need to apply this once daily, very hot weather sometimes requires a second application, later in the day. Shelf life is 9 to 12 months as long as water is not introduced to the jar.

Spring Detox Deodorant

This chemical-free deodorant is packed with three powerful springtime herbs that help promote lymph flow while soothing and softening the skin under your arms. Chickweed is a cooling herb that's sometimes used to treat benign cysts or swollen lymph glands. Violet leaves are often used in self-massage balms to treat fibrocystic breast disease. Dandelions are a classic spring tonic often taken internally, but also make lovely additions to deeply reparative salves, balms and other topical products. The herbs are infused in oil, then combined with shea butter and beeswax to thicken the product and to make it easier to apply. I've added arrowroot powder to keep you dry, along with kaolin clay to absorb sweat and odors. I chose a clean citrus blend for this deodorant, but you could substitute the listed essential oils with lavender or peppermint instead.

YIELD: 1 CUP (250 ML)

¼ cup (3 g) mixture of dried chickweed, violet leaves and dandelion flowers and leaves

2 tbsp (22 g) sunflower oil

½ cup (57 g) coconut oil

¼ cup (28 g) beeswax

¼ cup (52 g) shea butter

1 tbsp (6 g) white kaolin clay

1 tbsp (8 g) arrowroot powder

¼ tsp sweet orange essential oil

⅛ tsp grapefruit essential oil

4 drops frankincense essential oil (optional)

In a pint (500-ml) heatproof jar or container, combine the dried herbs and flowers, sunflower oil and coconut oil. Place the jar in a saucepan containing a few inches (at least 5 cm) of water, forming a makeshift double boiler. Heat over low heat for 2 hours, refilling the water as needed so the pot doesn't dry out. Remove the jar from the heat and strain into a wide-mouth pint (500-ml) canning jar or other glass mixing container.

Add the beeswax to the hot mixture and return to the saucepan. Heat over medium-low heat until the beeswax melts. Stir in the shea butter just until melted and remove from heat. Stir in the kaolin clay, arrowroot powder and essential oils.

Allow the deodorant to cool in the heating container, checking and stirring briskly every 5 minutes. Continue stirring frequently until it thickens and cools. Spoon the deodorant into glass jars and cover with their tops. Store in a cool, dry place out of direct sunlight. Shelf life is 9 to 12 months as long as water is not introduced to the jar.

Saint John's Wort, Arnica & Calendula Trauma Oil

Trauma oil is a classic remedy for aches, pains, bruises, minor sprains and tense muscles. It's made with a trio of powerful herbs: calendula, arnica and Saint John's wort, which act in synergy to calm inflammation and pain. Trauma oil can be used as massage oil, either alone or blended with essential oils, or incorporated into salves, creams and lotion bars. While I normally recommend infusing oils with dried herbs to reduce the risk of early spoilage, in the case of Saint John's wort, freshly gathered flowering tops are recommended. If you don't have fresh Saint John's wort flowers available, you can infuse the oil with calendula and arnica, and combine it with purchased Saint John's wort oil at a ratio of 2:1.

YIELD: 1 CUP (250 ML)

2 tbsp (2 g) dried arnica flowers

2 tbsp (2 g) dried calendula flowers

2 tbsp (2 g) fresh Saint John's wort flowering tops

1 cup (250 ml) sunflower, sweet almond or olive oil

Place the flowers and flowering tops in a pint (500-ml) canning jar. Pour the oil into the jar to cover the herbs.

Set the uncovered jar down in a saucepan containing 1 to 2 inches (2.5 to 5 cm) of water, then place the pan over a burner set to low. Keep the pan on the heat for around 2 hours to jump-start the infusing process.

Remove the pan from the heat and cover the jar with a piece of cheesecloth, a scrap of T-shirt or a coffee filter, secured by a rubber band. This protects the oil from dust and stray insects, but still allows breathing space for moisture from the fresh Saint John's wort to evaporate.

Set the jar in a sunny window to finish infusing for 3 to 4 weeks. Because the oil was made with fresh plant matter, it may develop a watery layer of sludge at the bottom of the jar. To make sure that unwanted sediment doesn't end up in your finished oil, strain the infused oil into a fresh jar, leaving behind as much of the bottom layer of sludgy oil as best as you can. Allow the oil to sit undisturbed for several days, then carefully decant into another clean, fresh jar, leaving any residue behind.

Because of the fresh plant infusion portion, I suggest storing the finished oil in the refrigerator and using within 9 months. If you purchased commercially made Saint John's wort oil, the shelf life can be extended to 1 year.

Lavender Dandelion Pain Relief Oil

A glass roll-on bottle makes it easy to apply this oil over achy joints, sore muscles and other areas in need of pain relief. Use a light oil that absorbs quickly into the skin for this recipe, such as sweet almond, grapeseed or apricot kernel oil. Tamanu oil is highly recommended for its anti-inflammatory properties, but if cost is an issue, it can be replaced with more sweet almond oil. Lavender calms and soothes sore muscles, while the mild analgesic properties of dandelion flowers offer relief from aches and pains.

YIELD: 4 OUNCES (120 ML) PAIN RELIEF OIL

½ cup (120 ml) sweet almond oil

¼ cup (9 g) dried lavender flowers

¼ cup (2 g) dried dandelion flowers

1 tbsp (15 ml) tamanu oil

2 to 3 drops lavender essential oil

Infuse the sweet almond oil with the dried lavender and dandelion flowers, using one of the methods on page 18.

Strain the finished oil, then add the tamanu oil and lavender essential oil.

Pour into glass roll-on bottles for easy application, or store in a half-pint (250-ml) jar and use as a massage oil.

Variation: Other herbs that work well in a pain relief oil include arnica flowers, comfrey leaf, comfrey root and goldenrod. If warmth makes your aches and pains feel better, you can also try adding a pinch of dried ginger to the infusing oils.

Lemon Balm & Ginger Sore Throat Drops

These herbal drops are a tasty way to soothe coughs and sore throats. Lemon balm is an amazing antiviral herb that also calms nervousness, promotes restful sleep and gently settles an upset stomach. Ginger is a beloved kitchen spice and powerful anti-inflammatory that's helpful for treating colds and flu, especially when chills, congestion, nausea and upset stomach are part of the symptoms.

YIELD: 3 TO 4 DOZEN

¾ cup (180 ml) water

½ tsp ground ginger

1 tbsp (1 g) fresh or dried lemon balm

½ cup (120 ml) honey

1 cup (200 g) granulated sugar

2 to 3 cups (250 to 375 g) confectioners' sugar

½ to ¾ tsp peppermint extract, to taste

In a small saucepan, heat the water to a simmer. Place the ground ginger and lemon balm in a half-pint (250 ml) jar and pour the simmering water over them. Cover with a saucer and steep for 30 to 40 minutes to make a strong herbal tea. Strain and measure out ½ cup (120 ml) of the tea to use in the recipe.

To a large, deep, stainless steel pot, add the ½ cup (120 ml) of herbal tea, honey and granulated sugar. Stir until evenly combined. Place the pot over a medium to medium-high burner, and bring to a boil. The candy will expand as it cooks, so you need the extra room of a taller pot to keep it from boiling over. Cook without further stirring until the mixture reaches 300°F (149°C) on a candy thermometer.

While the mixture cooks, prepare the powdered sugar molds by filling a large cookie sheet or cake pan with confectioners' sugar. Use something small, such as the top of the peppermint extract bottle, to make as many tiny indentions in the sugar as you can. Be sure to leave a little space between each one, so your sore throat drops don't all run together.

Once the candy mixture reaches the correct temperature, remove from heat and stir in the peppermint extract. At this point, I find it works best to quickly transfer the hot mixture to a 4-cup (1-L) Pyrex measuring cup with a pouring spout to make pouring easier.

Pour the hot candy mixture into the individual cavities of the powdered sugar mold, working quickly before it hardens in the pouring container. Allow the throat drops to cool completely, 30 to 40 minutes, then toss them around in the confectioners' sugar so they're fully coated. This will help with keeping them from sticking together. Store the sore throat drops in single layers between pieces of parchment paper in the refrigerator for up to 2 weeks, or freeze for longer storage for 4 to 6 months or more.

Bee Balm & Lemon Cough Syrup

Bee balm, also called wild bergamot, wild oregano and Oswego tea, is a potent herbal ally against colds, cough, sore throat and laryngitis. Here, it's combined with lemon zest for added flavor and infused into healing honey. We keep this on hand as a tasty way to treat sore or itchy throats year-round. If stomachache or a queasy feeling is part of your symptoms, bee balm is also an effective treatment for intestinal troubles, but you could stir a pinch of ground ginger into a spoonful of the infused honey, for added benefit. While this is a terrific home remedy for minor cold symptoms, if a sore throat persists or you have other concerning symptoms, be sure to consult with your health care provider for further advice. Medicinal amounts of bee balm remedies are not recommended during pregnancy.

YIELD: 11 OUNCES (312 G) INFUSED HONEY

¼ cup (2.8 g) dried bee balm flowers

Zest of 1 fresh lemon, grated

11 oz (312 g) honey

Place the bee balm flowers and lemon zest in a half-pint (250 ml) canning jar. Pour the honey over the top and stir with a chopstick or butter knife to release air bubbles. Cover with a lid and infuse in a sunny window for 2 weeks.

After infusing, you can choose to strain the honey through cheesecloth—a messy procedure that is helped by gently heating the honey no higher than 95°F (35°C), which is done by setting it in a small saucepan containing 1 to 2 inches (2.5 to 5 cm) of water placed over a low burner.

What I do more often is use a spoon to scoop off the top thick layer of herbs, pressing out as much honey as I can back into the jar as I do so. I then discard the honey-covered, spent flowers at the edge of our yard or some out-of-the-way spot to provide a happy discovery for ants and other little critters. When spooning out a dose of honey, I just pick through any stray bit of herb left in the jar.

Basil Mint Sore Throat Spray

Besides being a culinary superstar, basil has antibacterial, expectorant, sinus-opening and mild pain-relieving properties, making it a wonderful addition to this homemade sore throat spray. Here, it's paired with mint, for its refreshing taste and ability to cool and relieve inflammation. Raw honey is a powerful healer that helps coat and soothe painful throat tissue. The high concentration adds sweetness and helps preserve the herbal infusion longer than its normal shelf life of two days. For a mild throat-numbing effect and an extra boost against viruses, try adding echinacea or spilanthes tincture to your throat spray. The alcohol in the tincture will extend the shelf life by several additional weeks.

YIELD: 4 OUNCES (120 ML)

¼ cup (3 g) chopped fresh or frozen mint

2 to 3 fresh or frozen basil leaves

¼ cup (60 ml) boiling water

3 tbsp (45 ml) raw honey

Few drops of peppermint extract, for flavor

1 tbsp (15 ml) echinacea or spilanthes tincture (optional)

Place the mint and basil leaves into a heatproof mug or jar and pour the boiling water over them. Cover and steep for 20 minutes, then strain. Stir in the raw honey and a few drops of peppermint extract, if desired. Add the tincture, if using, and mix well.

Pour into a small spray bottle. Store in the refrigerator and use within 1 week, unless you added a tincture; then it should last for 3 to 4 weeks, if refrigerated between uses.

To use, shake well and spritz the spray once or twice into your mouth, aiming toward the back of your throat, as often as needed. If your sore throat persists or you feel increasingly worse, consult your health care provider.

Variation: For an extra antiviral boost, try adding lemon balm to this recipe. If you suffer from swollen tonsils, calendula flower may help as well. Keep in mind that calendula should not be taken internally by those who are pregnant.

Oregano Oxymel

Oxymels are tangy sweet and sour herbal syrups that are a traditional remedy for treating coughs and sore throats. Oregano is an antimicrobial powerhouse that's able to knock out a wide variety of germs. Apple cider vinegar is used as a tonic to promote health, and raw honey contains compounds that fight infection. Consider the amounts of vinegar and honey given below to be a flexible starting point; the ratios can be adjusted to suit your taste. Because the shelf life of oxymels is fairly long, try making a batch during the summer, when oregano is in season, and tuck it away for use during winter's cold and flu season.

YIELD: ²/₃ CUP (160 ML)

⅓ cup (5 g) chopped fresh oregano leaves

⅓ cup (80 ml) apple cider vinegar

⅓ cup (80 ml) raw honey

Place the chopped oregano in a half-pint (250-ml) canning jar. Pour the vinegar over the leaves and stir. Next, pour the honey into the jar and stir again. If you'd like a sweeter syrup, try using more honey than vinegar. If you prefer tangy, use more vinegar. Both honey and vinegar act as preservatives here, so you can't mess up this recipe by altering the amounts of either one.

Cap the jar with a nonmetallic lid and shake well. If you don't have a nonmetallic lid, place a sheet of wax paper or plastic wrap between the jar and lid, to prevent corrosion from the vinegar.

Set the oxymel aside for 2 to 3 weeks, to allow the flavors to meld and the benefits of oregano to infuse into the vinegar and honey. Strain and store in a cool, dark place. Shelf life is at least 1 year.

Take oxymels by the spoonful several times a day, or as needed, for sore throat, congested cough and the general discomforts of colds and flu. If your symptoms worsen or you have concerns, contact your health care provider.

Tip: Fresh oregano is ideal, but you can use dried if it's not available.

Variation: No oregano? Try basil or thyme instead.

Violet Flower Sore Throat Syrup

This tasty syrup gently helps to relieve the bothersome discomfort caused by the cough and sore throat that accompany minor colds. Violets are soothing, cooling and high in vitamin C, while raw honey is a natural antimicrobial that coats inflamed tissues.

YIELD: 1 CUP (250 ML)

½ cup (10 g) fresh or frozen violet flowers

½ cup (120 ml) boiling water

½ cup (120 ml) raw honey

Place the violet flowers in a heatproof pitcher or canning jar and pour the boiling water over them.

Allow the flowers to steep for around 1 hour, or until room temperature, then strain. At this point, the infusion should be a dark blue color. You can make your violet syrup right away or place the violet infusion in the refrigerator overnight. The flower infusion can also be frozen for 6 to 9 months, if you'd like to make some at a later time.

When ready to make your syrup, place the violet flower infusion in a small saucepan and gently heat until warm. Try to keep the temperature less than 110°F (43°C) in order to preserve all of the benefits of raw honey.

Remove the pan from heat and stir in the honey until completely incorporated. Pour into a glass bottle or jar with a tight-fitting lid.

To use, take 1 to 3 teaspoons (5 to 15 ml) of syrup every 3 or 4 hours, as needed, for minor coughs and sore throats, keeping in mind that violet is also a mild laxative. Store the sore throat syrup in the refrigerator and use within 2 weeks. You can also freeze individual doses in ice cube trays to extend the shelf life for use throughout the year. Simply thaw at room temperature and take the syrup as usual.

If your symptoms persist or worsen, check with a qualified health care provider.

Tip: Honey and honey-containing products should not be given to children under the age of 1 year old.

Cold Care Shower Steamers

These shower steamers are just the thing to help when stuffy noses and winter germs strike! Shower steamers are sometimes called shower bombs. They're made in a similar way to bath bombs, only without added oil or butter so the shower floor won't get slippery. Place one in the far corner of your shower where indirect splashes from the water spray will slowly dissolve it, releasing the therapeutic aroma while you wash up. Eucalyptus and tea tree were chosen for their ability to kill airborne influenza viruses, while eucalyptus and peppermint essential oils are excellent decongestants. These steamers have an essential oil dilution rate of 2 percent and are not designed for children under age 10 or for bathing. Use only in a shower. If you have household pets, especially cats, be sure to keep them away from the scented area to protect their health. For best results, make on a dry day with low humidity or in a room with a dehumidifier.

YIELD: 5 (2.9-OUNCE [84-G]) SHOWER STEAMERS

1 cup (286 g) baking soda

½ cup (118 g) citric acid

1 tbsp (6 g) white kaolin clay

¾ tsp eucalyptus essential oil

½ tsp peppermint essential oil

¼ tsp tea tree essential oil

Dishwashing gloves or latex or nitrile gloves

Witch hazel in a small spray bottle

¼-cup (60-ml) measuring cup

Dinner plate

Wax paper, cut into 6-inch (15-cm) squares

In a medium-sized mixing bowl, stir the baking soda, citric acid and clay together with a whisk, working out any clumps with your fingers. Sprinkle in the essential oils, and work it in while wearing gloves to avoid skin contact with undiluted essential oils.

Spray 1 to 2 light spritzes of witch hazel into the mixture while stirring with a whisk. Try squeezing a portion of the mixture into a ball shape. If it holds together without easily falling apart, it's ready to mold. If it crumbles, spray another spritz of witch hazel into the mixture while stirring and check again. The mixture is ready when it holds together easily without crumbling. Don't add too much witch hazel or your shower bombs will expand prematurely.

Fill the measuring cup with the shower steamer mixture, pressing firmly as you pack it in. Turn the dinner plate upside down on your work surface. Lay a square of wax paper on top, then turn out the shower steamer from the measuring cup and onto the wax paper. Gently slide the wax paper off the plate to the spot where you plan to let the steamers dry. Using the plate and wax paper in this way makes it much easier to move the steamers around. Allow them to air-dry for several hours, then wrap in airtight packaging.

Dandelion Magnesium Lotion

Experts posit that much of the population does not get enough magnesium in their daily diet. This can lead to headaches, leg cramps and a host of other subtle ailments. Besides baths with magnesium sulfate (Epsom salts) and magnesium supplements, another way to get more of this vital mineral is through the application of magnesium oil to the skin. Because the straight oil can be drying and irritating for some, it works well to couch it in a lotion or cream, especially ones containing soothing aloe. Dandelions were chosen for this recipe because the flowers have mild analgesic (pain-relieving) properties, making this cream especially helpful for leg cramps and other growing pains.

YIELD: 3½ OUNCES (105 ML)

2 tbsp (22 g) dandelion-infused oil (see page 18 for how to infuse oil)

3 tsp (6 g) emulsifying wax NF

2 tbsp (32 g) magnesium oil

2 tbsp (30 g) distilled water

1 tbsp (14 g) aloe vera gel

2 to 3 drops lavender essential oil (optional)

Preservative of choice (see tip)

Combine the dandelion-infused oil and emulsifying wax in a half-pint (250-ml) canning jar. In spite of its name, magnesium oil is actually water based so measure it out with the water and aloe and place in a separate half-pint (250-ml) jar. Cover that jar loosely with a canning lid to prevent water evaporation as it heats. Set both jars down in a small saucepan containing 1 to 2 inches (2.5 to 5 cm) of water. Place the pan over a medium-low burner until the wax is melted, about 15 minutes.

Remove from heat and carefully pour the two mixtures together. Stir briskly and frequently with a fork as the cream cools. Place the mixing container down in a bowl of ice water to speed up this step.

Once the cream has cooled below 104°F (40°C), stir in the essential oil, if using, and preservative. Pour the cream into glass jars or your preferred containers. Depending on your brand of emulsifying wax, the cream may take up to 24 hours to reach its final thickness.

Tip: For a nature-derived preservative option and shelf life of around 2 months, use 4 grams (1 tsp) of Leucidal SF Max to prevent bacteria plus 2 g (½ tsp) of AMTicide Coconut, to naturally prevent mold. For a longer shelf life of 6 to 9 months, use 1 g (¼ tsp) of Optiphen Plus, which is not considered all-natural, but is paraben-free and formaldehyde-free. If you choose to omit preservatives, store the cream in the refrigerator and use within 1 week.

Aloe Rose Sunburn & Hot Flash Spray

The calming, healing properties of rose shine in this fantastic spray that helps cool and ease the discomfort of sunburn and other flushed skin conditions. Witch hazel fights inflammation and heat, while aloe soothes and heals damaged skin. Apple cider vinegar is a traditional remedy for sunburn, so a small amount was added to this recipe. It doesn't really lend much smell, but if you're sensitive to the scent, use more witch hazel in its place. Storing the spray in the refrigerator adds an extra level of refreshing coolness and also helps extend the shelf life.

YIELD: 5 OUNCES (150 ML)

¼ cup (60 ml) witch hazel

¼ cup (60 ml) aloe vera gel

¼ cup (4 g) fresh rose petals

1 tbsp (15 ml) apple cider vinegar

1 tbsp (15 ml) water

Using a small food processor, blend all of the ingredients together until the mixture is light pink and frothy, with specks of rose petals visible. Strain.

Pour into a spray bottle and store in the refrigerator. Spritz on your neck, arms, legs and back as needed. You may also use this on your face; just make sure to close your eyes before spraying. If the spray does get into your eyes, simply flush with water.

This recipe utilizes the trick of blending flower petals with bottled aloe vera gel to extract their color and benefits, without the risk of early spoilage a simple rose water infusion would carry. It should keep well in your refrigerator for 1 month, or longer.

Chamomile Calming Syrup

This tasty syrup contains chamomile, a gentle herb that calms, relaxes and helps you unwind from a busy day. A touch of lemon balm is added, for its ability to soothe frayed nerves and to quiet the mind. Raw honey is a sweet-tasting product that acts as a preservative in this syrup. While both herbs are generally safe for most people, if you have health conditions, severe allergies or are pregnant or nursing, check with a health care provider before taking medicinal amounts of any herbs. Honey-containing products should not be given to children under the age of 1.

YIELD: 4 OUNCES (120 ML)

3 to 4 fresh or dried lemon balm leaves

1 tbsp (1 g) dried chamomile flowers or tea

¼ cup (60 ml) simmering hot water

¼ cup (60 ml) raw honey

Few drops of peppermint extract (optional)

Tear or crumble the lemon balm leaves into small pieces, then add them to a heatproof mug or jar along with the chamomile flowers. Pour the hot water over them and allow to steep for 45 minutes.

Strain and stir in the raw honey until dissolved. Add a few drops of peppermint extract for flavor, if you'd like.

Take 1 to 2 teaspoons (5 to 10 ml) several times a day, or as needed. You can also add it to a cup of hot tea. This syrup is especially good to take in the evening to promote a more restful sleep.

Store the finished syrup in your refrigerator. Shelf life is around 2 weeks. You can also freeze small amounts in ice cube trays for up to 6 months and thaw at room temperature, when needed.

Tip: If you're allergic to chamomile, try making this syrup with more lemon balm. Peppermint extract can be found in the baking and spice section of your local grocery store and is not to be confused with the much more potent peppermint essential oil.

Stress Relief Massage Oil

The demands of modern life can easily lead to chronic stress and mental exhaustion. It's important to set aside some time each day to give your nervous system a break and to recharge your batteries. This massage oil is infused with relaxing chamomile flowers, although lemon balm would be another nice choice. It's scented with a blend of lavender essential oil to calm and soften tension and mental stress. The lemon essential oil helps to alleviate negative thoughts and feelings of burnout. With a 1 percent dilution rate, this oil isn't designed for children under 6 years old.

YIELD: ³/₄ CUP (180 ML) MASSAGE OIL

¹/₄ cup (5 g) dried chamomile flowers

¹/₃ cup (78 ml) sweet almond or apricot kernel oil

¹/₃ cup (78 ml) sunflower oil

2 tbsp (30 ml) fractionated coconut or grapeseed oil

¹/₄ tsp lavender essential oil

¹/₈ tsp lemon essential oil

Place the dried chamomile in a pint (500-ml) canning jar. Add the sweet almond, sunflower and fractionated coconut oils. Infuse the oil using one of the methods on page 18.

Strain the oil into a clean jar and add the essential oils. Mix well. Cover and store the oil in a cool location, out of direct sunlight.

Use this oil for self-massage or have a partner apply it to tense neck and back muscles. It will help nourish and soften your skin as you enjoy a few relaxing moments!

Nontoxic Solutions for the Home

In this chapter, you'll learn how to ditch the store-bought toxins and their health-damaging side effects and to make your own simple but effective household cleaners, using just a few inexpensive ingredients from the grocery store, along with flowers and herbs from the garden.

These are great projects for using your more aromatic and antibacterial herbs, such as rosemary, sage, thyme and oregano. Roses and lavender add a soft and subtle scent to some of the recipes, but if you're not a fan of floral, try using citrus-scented herbs or zest in their place.

Make chore time safe for your kids by making up some Lemon Dusting Cloths (page 295) that contain no endocrine disruptors or persistent chemicals that will damage their long-term health, unlike the canned dusting sprays that line store shelves.

Skip the commercial disinfectant wipes, which are linked to respiratory and immune issues, and brew up an herbal vinegar spray (page 302) that has legendary disinfecting properties and is perfect for cleaning your home during cold and flu season.

Instead of spraying your windows with strongly scented blue sprays that can cause respiratory problems and skin irritation, try my pretty Rose Window Cleaner (page 301) for a streak-free shine that won't harm you, your family or the environment.

I also share recipes to naturally clean your laundry, counters, floors and more!

Lemon & Rosemary All-Purpose Cleaning Spray

I have a passion for infusing flowers and herbs into my everyday life, and I am always brainstorming new ways to use the plants that grow around me. One day it occurred to me that I'd never tried infusing liquid castile soap, so of course I had to experiment with the idea! I like how I can infuse the herbal benefits directly into the castile soap and then dilute it with plain water as needed, but this recipe would work fine with plain castile soap too, if you need to make up a batch of this cleaning spray more quickly. This is a great all-purpose spray with a clean, invigorating scent. I especially like using it for cleaning trash cans and baseboards.

YIELD: 1 CUP (250 ML) CLEANING SPRAY

1 tbsp (2 g) fresh or dried rosemary

1 tsp fresh lemon zest

⅓ cup (75 g) liquid castile soap, such as Dr. Bronner's

14 drops lemon essential oil

2 drops rosemary essential oil

1 cup (250 ml) distilled water

MAKE THE INFUSED CASTILE SOAP

Place the rosemary and lemon zest in a small glass jar. Pour the castile soap over and stir gently to combine. Cover the jar with a lid and place it in the refrigerator for 2 days to allow the rosemary and lemon to infuse into the soap. It's normal for the soap to turn cloudy when it's cold.

After 2 days, remove the infusing jar from the refrigerator and allow the soap to return to room temperature. Strain the soap through a fine mesh strainer into a clean jar. Store in the refrigerator for 3 weeks, or until needed.

MAKE THE CLEANING SPRAY

In a glass jar, combine 1 tablespoon (14 g) of infused soap and the essential oils. Gently stir in the distilled water and pour into a spray bottle.

Shake well before spraying over surfaces in need of cleaning such as trash cans, baseboards, bathroom counters and doorknobs. Be sure to spot test if you're unsure of its behavior on a particular surface.

Wipe the surface clean with absorbent rags or paper towels. Store leftover diluted cleaning spray in the refrigerator and use up within 3 days.

Lemon Thyme Dusting Spray

Those lemon-scented dusting sprays found in your local store's cleaning section may smell nice, but a quick glance at their labels shows products that are far from natural. Instead, try this simple and inexpensive recipe that's healthier for you and your furniture. The vinegar's purpose is to clean and cut through built-up grime, while the olive oil helps protect wood and leaves a nice shine behind. This spray can even help restore and improve the appearance of worn wooden surfaces! I chose lemon thyme for this recipe because it adds a disinfecting boost as it cleans, but you can mix and match whichever variety of lemon-scented herbs you like, such as lemon balm, lemon verbena and lemongrass.

YIELD: 3 OUNCES (90 ML) DUSTING SPRAY

1 lemon

1 cup (10 g) chopped fresh lemon thyme or other lemon-scented herbs

1 1/2 cups (375 ml) white vinegar

2 tbsp (30 ml) olive oil

Tip: If fresh herbs aren't available, you can use 1/2 cup (24 g) of dried instead.

FOR THE LEMON THYME VINEGAR

Remove the peel from the lemon and cut it into several pieces, or use a grater or zester. Try to get mostly colored zest, avoiding as much white pith as possible.

Place the lemon-scented herbs, pieces of lemon peel and white vinegar in a pint (500-ml) canning jar. Cover with a plastic lid. If you don't have a nonmetallic lid, place a few layers of wax paper or plastic wrap between the lid and jar, to keep the vinegar from corroding the metal.

Set the jar aside in a cupboard or other dark place for 1 to 2 weeks or until the vinegar smells distinctly of lemon. If needed, add more lemon peels and infuse a few weeks longer for a stronger scent. After sufficient time has passed, strain the vinegar into a clean jar. Label, cap and store out of sunlight.

The infused vinegar should last for around a year and can be used to make around 6 batches of dusting spray.

FOR THE DUSTING SPRAY

Combine 4 tablespoons (60 ml) of lemon herb vinegar with the olive oil in a small glass spray bottle. Shake well before and during each use, as the mixture tends to separate easily.

Spritz a small amount on a dusting rag and rub over dusty or worn wooden surfaces until they shine and the oil is evenly worked in. This spray can be used on furniture, tables, cabinet doors and other wooden surfaces, but isn't designed for hardwood floors.

Basic Toilet Bowl Cleaner

This simple recipe is effective for routine toilet cleaning. For tougher jobs, try adding ¼ cup (65 g) of super washing soda with the baking soda and use a pumice stone to scrub away persistent hard-water stains.

YIELD: 1 USE

½ cup (112 g) baking soda

½ cup (120 ml) Four Thieves Vinegar Spray (page 302)

Sprinkle the baking soda onto the sides and in the bowl of your toilet. Next, pour in the vinegar. It should immediately start bubbling up and fizzing. If not, try using ¾ to 1 cup each of baking soda (214 to 286 g) and vinegar (177 to 250 ml) the next time.

Using a toilet brush, scrub the bowl thoroughly, then flush.

Tip: Use a cotton ball moistened with hydrogen peroxide for lightening stains on and around the toilet lid.

Lemon Balm Furniture Polish

While you can rub your furniture directly with lemon balm leaves for a fresh scent and shine, it takes a lot of leaves, time and patience to do so. Instead, try drying your lemon balm leaves and infusing them into an oil that has a long shelf life, such as jojoba, coconut or olive, then turn that into a homemade polish that makes your wooden surfaces gleam!

YIELD: 1 OUNCE (28 G)

1 tbsp (1 g) dried lemon balm leaves, crumbled

1 oz (30 ml) jojoba oil

0.15 oz (4 g) beeswax

Lemon essential oil, optional

Place the dried lemon balm leaves and jojoba oil in a half-pint (250-ml) canning jar. Set the jar down in a saucepan containing 1 to 2 inches (2.5 to 5 cm) of water. Heat over a burner set to low for 1 hour, then strain oil into a 4-ounce (120-ml) canning jar. You can save a little bit of cleanup time by using this half-pint (250-ml) jar for both mixing together and storing the furniture polish.

Weigh out the beeswax directly into the jar with the strained oil, then set it in the saucepan you used to infuse the jojoba oil. Turn heat to medium-low and heat until the beeswax is completely melted. Remove from heat. If desired, stir in a few drops of lemon essential oil, for scent and added cleaning power.

Using scraps of old T-shirts or other soft rags, rub a small amount into your wooden furniture, rolling pins and cutting boards as needed. Follow with a buffing using a clean rag.

Rose Window Cleaner

Brighten up chore time with this pretty pink window cleaner made from fresh roses. It utilizes the natural grease- and grime-cutting abilities of white vinegar. Cornstarch may sound like an odd ingredient, but its specific purpose in the recipe is to help prevent streaking. For the most beautiful, streak-free shine, try using this spray in conjunction with crumpled newspaper or bird's-eye cotton (the material that diaper flats are made of).

YIELD: ENOUGH TO FILL A 2-OUNCE (60-ML) SPRAY BOTTLE

1 cup (10 g) fresh pink or red rose petals

1½ cups (375 ml) white vinegar

2 tbsp (30 ml) water

Pinch of cornstarch

FOR THE ROSE-INFUSED VINEGAR

Place the rose petals and vinegar in a pint (500-ml) canning jar. Cover with a plastic or nonmetallic lid. If you don't have one, place a few layers of plastic wrap or wax paper over the jar before putting the lid on, to keep the vinegar from corroding the metal.

Set the jar aside in a cool, dark place for 1 to 2 weeks, or until the vinegar turns pink and takes on a light rose scent. If you'd like a stronger smell, add more rose petals and infuse for another week. Strain the finished vinegar into a clean jar. Label, cap and store out of direct sunlight. The color will fade over time, but the vinegar will remain usable for at least 1 year, or longer.

FOR THE ROSE WINDOW CLEANER

Pour 2 tablespoons (30 ml) of rose-infused vinegar into a small spray bottle. Add the water and cornstarch and shake well.

Spritz on windows, mirrors and other glass surfaces, then wipe off with crumpled newspaper or bird's-eye cotton. Vinegar can damage or cause etching on granite, stone or marble, so avoid using on those types of surfaces.

Tip: It's easy to scale up this recipe to make larger quantities. Just combine equal parts of water and vinegar, plus a pinch of cornstarch.

Four Thieves Vinegar Spray

There is an old legend of four thieves who went around robbing the homes and graves of those who had been stricken by the plague during medieval times. The mystery of why they never got sick themselves was solved when they were finally captured and gave up their secret in exchange for pardons of their crimes. They claimed to have steeped a special blend of herbs in vinegar, then soaked rags in it to cover their faces and to wash with during and after their nefarious acts. Whether such a band of thieves actually existed or not may never be known, but scientific research today tells us that many aromatic herbs do indeed have strong disinfecting and antimicrobial properties.

I like to make up a large batch of this vinegar each year to keep on hand for use during cold and flu season. It's great for cleaning surfaces such as sinks, light switches, toilet seats, refrigerator handles and other places germs might lurk. While there may have been only four thieves in the legend, you're not limited to using just four herbs in this recipe. The original formulas that sprang up around that time were thought to contain many herbs, for the widest array of benefits possible.

YIELD: 1½ CUPS (375 ML)

¼ cup (3 to 4 g) each of chopped fresh rosemary, mint, lavender leaves, sage, thyme and oregano, 1½ cups (18 to 24 g) total

Few whole cloves (optional)

1½ cups (375 ml) vinegar

Water for diluting

Place the herbs in a pint (500-ml) canning jar. Some variations of the recipe contain cloves, for their potent germ-fighting properties. If you like their scent, try adding a few to the jar. Pour the vinegar over the herbs. Add extra vinegar, if needed, to ensure that the herbs are fully covered.

Cover with a nonmetallic lid or place a few layers of wax paper or plastic wrap between the jar and metal lid, to prevent corrosion from the vinegar.

Set the vinegar in a dark place to infuse for 1 to 2 weeks. Strain and store in a glass jar. Shelf life is at least 1 year.

To use, dilute with equal parts of water, and spray on soiled or germy areas, then wipe off with old rags or paper towels. Vinegar can damage or cause etching on granite, stone or marble, so avoid using on those types of surfaces.

Tip: If you don't have fresh herbs, try using half as much dried herbs instead.

Orange Pine Floor Cleaner

The grime-fighting powers of citrus combine with the disinfecting woodsy scent of pine in this basic floor cleaner recipe for no-wax, laminate and ceramic tile flooring. Avoid using on hardwood floors, as the acid in vinegar may damage finishes over time.

YIELD: 1½ CUPS (375 ML) FLOOR CLEANER

½ cup (12 g) chopped pine needles

Zest or peelings from 1 orange

1½ cups (375 ml) white vinegar

Place the pine needles and orange zest in a pint (500-ml) jar. It doesn't matter if you have a large or small orange; there's no precise amount needed for this recipe.

Pour the vinegar into the jar. Add extra, if needed, to cover all of the plant material. Cap with a nonmetallic lid. If one isn't available, place a few layers of plastic wrap or wax paper between the jar and lid, to prevent corrosion from the vinegar.

Tuck the vinegar away in a dark cupboard for 1 to 2 weeks, then strain.

If you'd like a stronger scent, fill a new jar with a fresh supply of pine needles and orange peel, and pour the freshly strained vinegar on top. Repeat the 1- to 2-week waiting time to create a double-strength infusion.

To use, mix ¼ to ½ cup (60 to 120 ml) of orange pine floor cleaner into a gallon (3.8 L) of hot water and mop as usual.

Lavender Laundry Detergent

It's so easy to make your own laundry detergent! This project calls for the Coconut Laundry Soap & Stain Stick recipe found on page 251. If you're unable to make your own, look for natural laundry soap bars in your local grocery or health food store. I like to add a small amount of sweet-scented lavender to my detergent, but you can use another herb, such as lemongrass, instead, or leave the herbs out completely.

YIELD: 16 TO 24 LOADS OF LAUNDRY

1 bar homemade Coconut Laundry Soap (page 251)

1 1/2 to 2 cups (405 to 540 g) super washing soda

1/4 cup (6 g) dried lavender (optional)

1/2 to 1 tsp lavender essential oil (optional)

1/4 to 1/2 cup (60 to 120 ml) Lavender Fabric Softener (page 308) per laundry load (optional)

Using an inexpensive box grater, grate the bar of soap. You should end up with about 1 1/2 cups (75 g) of grated soap.

Place the soap flakes in the bowl of a food processor. Add the super washing soda.

Using an electric coffee grinder or mortar and pestle, pulverize the lavender, then rub it through a fine mesh sieve, so that a fine powder results. This should yield around 1 tablespoon (1 g) of powder. Add the lavender powder to the food processor.

Pulse the soap flakes, super washing soda and lavender powder until it's completely mixed, with no visible flakes of soap remaining. Stir in the lavender essential oil, if using.

Pour into a glass jar, label and close tightly. Use 2 to 3 tablespoons (26 to 39 g) per load of laundry, along with the fabric softener in the fabric softener dispenser, if using. If you don't have any of the Lavender Fabric Softener made up, you can use plain vinegar as a softener.

Tip: Depending on the size and shape of your soap bar, you may end up with more or less grated soap, and the recipe easily can be adapted to accommodate. For every 1/2 cup (25 g) of grated soap, you'll need 1/2 cup (135 g) of super washing soda.

Fresh Mint Wall Wash

The uplifting smell of mint refreshes and energizes, while natural castile soap lifts and washes away the grime and sticky fingerprints that tend to collect on household walls and doors. If you don't have fresh mint, try using half as much dried.

YIELD: 2¹/₂ CUPS (625 ML)

1 cup (14 g) fresh mint leaves

1¹/₂ cups (375 ml) simmering hot water

1 cup (250 ml) cold water

1 tsp liquid castile soap

Peppermint essential oil (optional)

Place the mint leaves in a heatproof jar or pitcher. Pour the simmering hot water over the leaves. Let this steep for 20 minutes, then strain.

Combine the strained mint tea with the cold water, then gently stir in the castile soap and 1 to 2 drops peppermint essential oil, if using.

Use old rags to dip in the solution and wipe down walls, doors and window frames. Make up only enough wall wash that you can use at once; it doesn't store well beyond 1 day.

Lavender Fabric Softener

Vinegar is one of the most frugal fabric softeners around. It helps to remove leftover detergent and softens your clothing as it does so. While lavender is a favorite at our house because of its tick-repelling properties and sweet scent, try infusing your vinegar with a variety of your favorite flowers, herbs and citrus zest to brighten up your laundry routine.

YIELD: ENOUGH FOR AROUND 6 LOADS OF LAUNDRY

²/₃ cup (24 g) dried lavender flowers

1¹/₂ cups (375 ml) white vinegar

Combine the lavender flowers and white vinegar in a pint (500-ml) jar. Cap with a nonmetallic lid and let steep for 1 to 2 weeks, out of direct sunlight. If you have only metal lids, place a few sheets of plastic wrap or wax paper between the jar and lid, to prevent corrosion from the vinegar.

Strain the finished vinegar. It will have turned a pretty shade of pink at this point and carry the faint scent of lavender. If you'd like a stronger floral smell, fill a new jar with a fresh supply of dried lavender flowers and pour the freshly strained vinegar on top. Repeat the infusion process for another 1 to 2 weeks, then strain again.

To use, add around ¹/₄ cup (60 ml) to the fabric softener dispenser on your machine or use a dispenser ball, available in the laundry section of your local supermarket. You may find that you need up to ¹/₂ cup (120 ml) if you have hard water.

Natural Wax Melts

Commercial wax melts are loaded with synthetic fragrances that can often be problematic for those of us with allergies, asthma or chemical sensitivities. These DIY versions are made with beeswax and coconut oil, naturally colored and scented with essential oils. Keep in mind that cats are sensitive to fragranced items and essential oils, so avoid using these wax melts around them. The suggested essential oil amounts are calculated at 5 percent and based on the IFRA category 11 safe rates for candles and air-freshener products, per the results at EOCalc.com. When a wax melt first starts heating, you may not smell the essential oil right away, but give it time to start melting and then you will!

YIELD: 8 TO 12 WAX MELTS, DEPENDING ON MOLD SIZE

½ cup plus ½ tbsp (106 g) coconut oil

Natural colorant from the list below

¼ cup (28 g) beeswax

Essential oil from the list below

TO MAKE THE INFUSED COCONUT OIL

In a pint (500-ml) canning jar or other heatproof container, combine the coconut oil and natural colorant. If you'd like to minimize speckles in the final product, secure the colorant in a heat seal-style tea bag first. Set the container down in a small saucepan containing 1 to 2 inches (2.5 to 5 cm) of water, then place the pan over a low burner for 1 hour to allow the color to infuse into the coconut oil.

TO MAKE THE MELTS

Strain the infused coconut oil into a new container. I use a dedicated jar for beeswax-based projects, or you may want to use an upcycled soup can for easy cleanup. Add the beeswax to the infused coconut oil, and place the jar or can in the small saucepan of water used to infuse the oil. Refill the water if needed, so the pot doesn't dry out during heating. Heat over a medium-low burner until the wax melts, 30 to 40 minutes.

Remove from heat and let cool for 5 minutes. Stir in the essential oil and pour the melted wax mixture into small silicone or candy molds. Placing the molds on a cookie sheet makes it easier to move them around without spilling hot wax. Leave the melts in the mold for 2 to 3 days, then remove and store in glass jars.

NATURAL COLORANT OPTIONS

⅛ tsp indigo powder (blue)

½ tsp chlorella powder (green)

⅛ tsp alkanet root powder (pink)

¼ tsp annatto seed powder (orange)

SUGGESTED ESSENTIAL OILS

5% usage rate, or 7 g (~¾ tsp) each

7 g (~¾ tsp) Peppermint

7 g (~¾ tsp) Cedarwood Himalayan

7 g (~¾ tsp) Pink grapefruit

7 g (~¾ tsp) Lavender

7 g (~¾ tsp) Sweet orange

All-Natural Pet Care

Pets can enjoy the benefits of herbs and flowers too! In this chapter we'll make a minty fresh treat to help banish dog breath, along with another tasty, vitamin-rich treat that dogs and cats alike will enjoy.

If your pet is always scratching because of pesky fleas, try making some herbal flea powder (page 319), or soothe their skin with a simple herbal rinse (page 320) after their bath.

I also share the all-purpose first-aid salve recipe (page 323) that I use on everyone from my goats to my chickens to my dogs. It's great for using on humans too!

One of my all-time favorite recipes is a broth-based tinkle tonic (page 328) that I designed especially for my senior dachshund that had increasing accidents in the house as she aged. This tonic made a world of difference for her and decreased the amount of accidents to almost none. If you have a dog with an excitable bladder and their vet has ruled out serious conditions and deemed them otherwise healthy, you may find it helpful as well!

Our pets offer companionship, entertainment and unconditional love. For many households, they're also valued members of the family. Why not make them their own natural and nontoxic products too?

Yarrow & Bee Balm Antiseptic Wash

A vet should be consulted for serious injuries, but this antiseptic herbal wash is useful for treating hot spots and minor scrapes and wounds at home. I've also found it helpful for treating the acne that my rescue bulldog boxer mix is prone to. Bee balm is antimicrobial, antifungal and helps relieve itching, while yarrow disinfects and stops bleeding. Yarrow also has the bonus effect of repelling fleas and mosquitoes. Both herbs are considered safe for cats and dogs, although yarrow should be used with caution with pregnant or nursing animals. This wash is to be used externally and applied directly to the problem spot.

YIELD: 1 CUP (250 ML)

¼ cup (2 g) dried bee balm, or about 7 dried flower heads

1 tbsp (2.5 g) dried yarrow

1 cup (250 ml) distilled water

Place the bee balm and yarrow in a pint (500-ml) canning jar. Heat the water to a simmer, then pour into the jar to cover the herbs. Cover the jar with a saucer and steep the tea for 45 to 60 minutes, or until it's lukewarm.

Strain the tea into a clean jar. Store the antiseptic wash in the refrigerator for up to 3 days. For longer storage, freeze in ice cube trays until solid, then store the frozen cubes in a freezer container for 5 to 6 months.

To use, remove a cube from the freezer as needed. It can be thawed overnight in the refrigerator, or gently heated in a small saucepan until melted. Bring to room temperature before using on your pup. If your pet isn't scared of spray bottles, the tea can be directly spritzed onto the trouble spot. If your pet finds spray bottles scary, soak a cotton ball in the tea and gently dab over the affected area.

Flea-Repelling Vinegar Rinse

This rinse is helpful to use on your dog near the end of their bath. The vinegar removes soap residue while the yarrow and oxeye daisies add a punch against fleas. Lavender, plantain and calendula are all skin-soothing herbs; you could use just one of them, or combine the three. Cats don't generally require baths, but you could sparingly and occasionally use this on them if the calendula is omitted.

YIELD: ENOUGH FOR 12 RINSES

½ cup (8 to 10 g) combined mixture of dried yarrow, oxeye daisies, lavender, plantain and/or calendula in roughly equal parts

1½ cups (375 ml) apple cider vinegar, plus more if needed

½ cup (120 ml) water

Place the herbs in a pint (500-ml) canning jar. Pour the vinegar into the jar. Add more vinegar, if needed, to ensure the herbs are completely covered.

Cap the jar with a plastic lid, or place a layer of parchment paper between the jar and a metal lid, to prevent corrosion. Tuck the jar away in a cool, dark place for 3 to 4 weeks. Strain the infused vinegar and compost the spent herbs.

Store the vinegar undiluted for 1 to 2 years. When you need to make a rinse, combine 1 to 2 tablespoons (15 to 30 ml) of infused vinegar with ½ cup (120 ml) of comfortably warm water.

Bathe your dog as normal, then pour the rinse over them, covering as much of their fur as possible, but avoiding their eyes and ears. Do not wash the rinse off their skin with plain water; instead, allow it to stay on for the most effectiveness. Dry with a towel.

Itchy Skin Rinse

This after-bath rinse is designed to help relieve and soothe your dog's itchy skin. Cats don't often require or appreciate bathing, so this recipe wasn't created with them in mind. Dill provides limonene, a compound with flea-killing properties, while calendula, rose and lavender flowers help calm irritation and inflammation. The antiseptic action of yarrow makes it a good addition if your pet has scratched raw spots on their skin. Yarrow may also help repel fleas. While this rinse can offer temporary relief, if your dog has chronic skin issues, you may want to investigate whether something in their diet is the culprit.

YIELD: 2½ CUPS (625 ML)

1½ to 2 cups (375 to 500 ml) apple cider vinegar

1½ cups (18 to 24 g) of the following:

Fresh dill

Calendula flowers

Yarrow

Lavender

Rose petals and leaves

1 cup (250 ml) warm water

Heat the vinegar to a gentle simmer.

Fill a 1-quart (1-L) canning jar halfway with as many of the herbs and flowers that you have on hand. While fresh dill is optimal, it's fine if the other ingredients are dried, if that's what's available to you.

Cover the flowers and herbs with the hot apple cider vinegar. Let cool to a comfortable temperature, then strain into a mixing bowl or pitcher. Add the warm water and pour over your dog as a final rinse after their bath.

Peppermint & Parsley Fresh-Breath Dog Treats

This cool treat combines fresh peppermint and parsley to help bust the bad-breath germs that often plague our dogs. Be sure to use plain, unsweetened yogurt in this recipe, as sugar isn't going to help the situation any. It's important to avoid artificial sweeteners and xylitol as well, because those can be quite toxic to our canine buddies.

YIELD: 12 TO 24 TREATS

1 cup (227 g) plain yogurt

2 tbsp (5 g) chopped parsley

2 tbsp (5 g) chopped fresh mint

1 drop pure peppermint extract (optional)

Blend all of the ingredients together in a small food processor. Divide the mixture evenly between the compartments of an ice cube tray. If you have a small-breed dog, make smaller portions and divide between two trays.

Freeze until solid, then remove from the tray. Store the cubes in a freezer bag and keep frozen until use.

Some dogs might not like the hard texture, but they may like the softness of a treat that's been thawed in the refrigerator for several hours.

If your dog has persistent bad breath, an examination of their diet and a checkup at the vet are probably in order to rule out any underlying health conditions.

Nettle & Coconut Oil Vitamin Treats

These tasty treats feature nettle, which is loaded with vitamins and trace minerals, and coconut oil, for its ability to reduce itchiness and to promote healthy skin and shiny coats. They are suitable to give to both dogs and cats. Grass-fed butter is an optional healthy add-in for pets that might not like the taste of straight coconut oil.

YIELD: 12 TO 24 SMALL TREATS

$^{1}/_{2}$ cup (100 g) unrefined coconut oil

$^{1}/_{4}$ cup (3 g) dried nettle leaves

4 tbsp (56 g) grass-fed butter (optional)

Infuse the coconut oil with nettles, using the quick method on page 19, and then strain.

Pour the strained nettle-infused coconut oil into tiny silicone molds. Plastic ice cube trays can be used for larger dog breeds and can be filled halfway, so the treats aren't too large.

Place the molds in the refrigerator until they firm up. Remove the treats from the mold and store in a tightly closed jar or container in your refrigerator; they get too soft at room temperature. These make perfect bite-size treats that can be given directly from the refrigerator.

If you have a picky dog that isn't fond of the taste of straight coconut oil, try mixing in $^{1}/_{2}$ tablespoon (7 g) of melted butter per 1 tablespoon (12 g) of coconut oil, and making the treats with that combination instead.

Remember, even though these are healthy treats, you can still overfeed your pets. I give just 1 per day to my miniature dachshund and cats, while my larger-breed dogs get 2 or 3. If your pet has pancreatitis or trouble digesting fats, consult with your veterinarian for their advice.

Tinkle Tonic Broth

I created this herbal broth for my littlest dog, a senior dachshund that had increasing trouble with accidents in the house as she aged. Corn silk, the fine threads you find on an ear of fresh corn when shucking it, is an anti-inflammatory that's often used for incontinence and bedwetting in humans and pets alike. Marshmallow root protects and lubricates the urinary tract. Nettle is a vitamin-rich tonic herb, and astragalus root strengthens overall immunity and kidney circulation. Another good addition for short-term use could include purple coneflower (echinacea) as an antimicrobial to prevent infection. These herbs are steeped in homemade chicken broth—made with only chicken, water, carrots and a small dash of Redmond Real Salt, then strained. It makes a tasty healing broth that my dog just loves to take! Combined with taking her on more frequent walks, it helped a great deal. Before trying home remedies such as this one, be sure to first visit your dog's vet to rule out potentially serious conditions or infections that are causing the symptoms.

YIELD: 2 CUPS (500 ML) BROTH

2 cups (500 ml) plain chicken broth

1 tbsp (3 g) fresh or 2 tsp (1 g) dried corn silk

2 tsp (3 g) chopped dried marshmallow root

2 tsp (1 g) dried nettle leaf

2 tsp (4 g) dried astragalus root

In a small saucepan, bring the broth just to a simmer. Remove from heat.

In a pint (500-ml) jar, place the corn silk, marshmallow root, dried nettle leaf and astragalus root. Pour the hot broth over the herbs and cover with a saucer. Steep for 15 minutes, then strain into a clean jar.

Store the broth in the refrigerator for up to 3 days. For longer storage, freeze in ice cube trays until solid, then store the frozen cubes in a freezer container for up to 6 months. Remove a cube from the freezer as needed. It can be thawed overnight in the refrigerator, or gently heated in a small saucepan until melted. Let the hot broth cool before giving it to your pet.

My dog is a small breed, less than 15 pounds (6.8 kg), and I give her about 1 to 2 tablespoons (15 to 30 ml) of broth twice a day. I often pour it over her food, but she likes it served alone too.

About the Author

Jan Berry is a writer, herbalist, soap maker and owner of the website The Nerdy Farm Wife. The first edition of this book was published as *101 Easy Homemade Products for Your Skin, Health and Home* in 2016. She's also the author of *Simple & Natural Soapmaking* and *Easy Homemade Melt & Pour Soaps*. She lives in the Blue Ridge Mountains of Virginia with her family, where she enjoys collecting weeds and finding fun things to make with them. She's also an avid reader and enjoys nothing more than a good book and a cozy fire, with a purring kitty or snoring dog nearby.

Index